THE SEVENTH AGE
OF MANAGEMENT

by
Keith Stanton

authorHOUSE®

AuthorHouse™
1663 Liberty Drive, Suite 200
Bloomington, IN 47403
www.authorhouse.com
Phone: 1-800-839-8640

First published by AuthorHouse 7/23/2007

ISBN: 978-1-4343-1354-6 (sc)

Printed in the United States of America
Bloomington, Indiana

This book is printed on acid-free paper.

Table of Contents

Prologue

T he members of Votive have, collectively, spent many years providing a coaching service to professional organisations of every shape and size. Like most people in our field, we are aware that it is past time we all started making some serious changes to the way we live and work.

What follows is our analysis of the situation, and our suggestions as to how we can all work together to make tomorrow's organisations friendlier, more adaptable, more efficient and more successful.

We call this approach the "Votive Process."

Keith Stanton

PART ONE:

THE WAY WE WERE/
THE WAY WE ARE

Chapter 1)

The Seven Ages of Management

*Those who cannot learn from history are doomed
to repeat it*—George Santayana

It has long been a source of surprise to me that business people are
given very little background to the development of management studies.
Instead, we are taught management in a very dogmatic way—"This
is how it is done!"—as if we were being instructed in the fundamentals
of some particularly intransigent religion rather than a dynamic, living
element of existence that should and could change as we do. The impression
is that "this" is how management has always been done and, indeed, that
there is *no other way*. It is almost as if the "rules" of management that
we have absorbed from our first day on the job simply came into being
organically; as if they were natural laws as immutable as the law of gravity.
Nobody questions the fundamentals of management; not managers, not
employees and rarely even consultants. We accept that the fundamentals
are a given, and attempt to work at changing no more than the surface of
our behaviour.

We know the names of great thinkers in fields such as science and
technology—who has not heard of Einstein and Pasteur, Bell and Gates?—
but few of us can name the people who formed modern management
systems. I believe that this is at the heart of the problems that managers
and management theorists are facing today.

Well, guess what? There is more than one way to manage. We do not have to continue to live and work with a system that has largely outlived its usefulness. We can find a new way, one that reflects modern modes of living, working and being, and results in a far more efficient outcome for both arenas of existence.

The fact is that it is time to consider tearing up our rule book and starting from scratch. Society has changed, technology has changed and certainly industry, manufacturing and service have all changed too. Why has management not followed suit? That is a good question. In fact, when it comes to corporate culture, resistance to change is as ingrained as it is imperfectly understood. Unaware of the possibilities for difference, managers are stuck with what they know. Afraid of the challenges that accompany change and stuck with a mindset that sees every challenge as a potential failure, they think that it is easier to continue with a tried and tested formula, despite the fact that the results—widespread unhappiness in the workplace, massive problems with talent retention and underperforming businesses—should speak for themselves.

Bearing in mind the axiom that one has to know the past in order to understand the present and create a better future, let us start our exploration with a review of the history of management as we know it today.

The first age of management: If it runs, we can eat it.

All human societies organise themselves, regardless of where they are and how they make their living. This organisation is part of what makes us human, and makes possible any endeavour more complex than rooting around in the ground for an edible root to chew on. Without organisation, there is no society, and without society we would not be human at all. In his 1999 publication, The Hunting Apes, Stanford argues the case for the evolution of human intelligence on the basis of the need to organise: "...the origins of human intelligence are linked to the acquisition of meat, especially through the cognitive capacities necessary for the strategic meat sharing with fellow group members. Important aspects of the behaviour of some higher primates—hunting and meat sharing and the social and cognitive skills that enable these behaviours...point to the origins of human intelligence."

In other words, the necessity of organising themselves so as to provide for themselves created the situation in which our ancestors began to evolve into a more intelligent type of being; into *us*. In fact, one of the current theories about why human beings superseded Neanderthals bases its case on the division of labour. According to this theory, the division of work into different activities suited to different people—food preparation, gathering of plants and small game and childcare to women and hunting and scouting activities to men, for example—could have given Homo Sapiens an edge over Neanderthals, if the latter engaged all the members of a group in any given activity at any given time, thus exposing everyone in the group to danger.

So there you have it: our very existence probably owes a lot to the application of management.

In the world today, while human *beings* are all equally complex, human *societies* are extremely varied with different levels of organisational complexity. The simplest cell of society is a small tribal set-up, as found in earlier stages of cultural development in the West and among some modern hunter-gatherer societies and the most complex to date is seen in modern industrial society, with its multiple forms of authority and an infinite number of methods of interaction. Broadly speaking, these units have a lot in common with the organisational needs of, respectively, large and small companies today.

In simple societies, everybody works to sustain the group, which functions in a manner not completely unlike that of a small commercial organisation. A typical division of labour would see the men leaving periodically to engage in hunting or fishing, while women devote themselves to gathering food crops, skinning and preparing the animals brought in from the hunt and taking care of children and other dependents. In certain seasons, or when they were not otherwise occupied, people would take care of things such as weapon and tool manufacture, maintenance of the camp and so forth. Clearly, none of this could take place without organisation. A common organisational environment in this sort of society would involve a chief or "Big Man" who oversees things at a macro level, often with the help of the local religious leader, while on a smaller scale, defined roles in hunting, gathering, food preparation and childcare emerge with local leadership figures who coordinate, more or less formally, what is being done. Some scholars believe that speech and the ability to engage in abstract thought gradually emerged as a result of human's relatively weak bodies and need to organise themselves in groups so as to provide themselves with all the nutrients they required. Small-scale societies are often intensely conservative, and resist change vigorously, sometimes even punishing transgressors from the local norm with terrible fates.

The second age of management: Bringing it all back home

So far, so simple. Then, of course, agriculture was developed in various parts of the world, and societies became more complex, with the result that roles became more specific and social organisation more complicated. Before, hunter gatherers were typically nomadic, and would move on when they felt that they had exhausted the resources of an area for the time being (as modern hunter-gatherers do today). Socially, they were also very egalitarian, at least within groups. The tribal identity was foremost. Other tribes might have been seen as inferiors, but within the group enterprises were carried out and shared with all of the group's members.

With agriculture, people settled down. They started to invest a great deal, practically and emotionally, into their specific area. The work they did one year would have ramifications for the success of next year's endeavours, and so on. Some people became wealthier than others. Some areas produced some but not all of the group's needs. Some tribes became wealthier than others, and some decided that they wanted more and engaged in conquering and subduing their neighbours. As a result of all of this, a more complex form of commerce emerged and, by as early as the Bronze Age, a surprisingly lively import/export system was in action all over Europe (we will choose all our examples from Europe and the United States, as this is where our focus is). Societies that were socially stratified appointed very specific roles to specific types of people; there were farmers and bureaucrats, artisans and traders. In response to these changes in livelihood, society and social norms became more complex and so did ways of administering society and organising work. Because food now had to be harvested in certain seasons, and stored in others, for example, some individuals became specialists in areas such as ceramic manufacture, enabling the long-term storage of foodstuffs, while others engaged in food preparation, warfare and so forth. As territories grew, overseeing them became too much for just one centralised authority to manage, and a series of lesser authorities developed to maintain supply of foods and other crucial matters.

The third age of management: the centralisation of authority

By the Middle Ages, the social system that had emerged was what we now refer to as "feudal". To put it in a nutshell, this system had a lot going for it…if you happened to be at the top of the heap, that is! Local rulers oversaw their territories and the people who lived in them fulfilled their specific roles as peasants, tailors, blacksmiths and what have you with very little opportunity to do anything else. Typically, sons and daughters grew up to do exactly what their parents had done before them, with little or no scope for doing anything else. Taxes were paid in the form of a percentage of whatever the peasants managed to produce and most lives were effectively owned by somebody else and ultimately by the King, whose right to rule was derived from heredity and often justified in the form of rather dubious mythological precedents (the questioning of which was typically a capital offence). When the King or local authority decided to go to war, the people had to serve as soldiers and hand over a hefty percentage of what they managed to grow to the army and state. The promised rewards tended to be a little vague. The faithful and the virtuous might get a place in Heaven when their rather short and miserable lives came to an end, which must have sounded good to the unfortunate peasants of the time. Those who digressed, however, faced severe, often capital, punishment, which also served as a frequent reminder to those left behind that resistance to the status quo was futile. In these days, there was no division between the state and the church or the state and the military apparatus, and both church and army functioned in society much like board members of an old-fashioned company, of which the CEO was the King, and the heads of departments his various fiefs.

The fourth age of management: when industry ruled

Let's fast forward to the Industrial Revolution. This was the period during the eighteenth and nineteenth centuries when machines—first in Britain and gradually elsewhere in the developed world—began to enter the production function in a big way, making large scale production possible and changing the way of working dramatically. First textile manufacturing was mechanised, followed by rapid advances in the creation of iron, and the building of a network of canals, roads and railways alongside the industrial application of steam power. More people flocked to towns and cities to work, leaving the countryside behind and prompting in turn the emergence of more scientific, less labour-intensive forms of agriculture. Whereas before, textiles, metal goods and so on were laboriously made one by one by individual artisans in their workshops, now they were made much more quickly and effectively in factories, with machines performing more and more of the essential work. Human labour was, however, still crucial. Men, women and child workers were an integral part of the production process. They were motivated to keep working by fear of losing their job, of losing an eye or limb to the dangerous production process and by fear of the boss who could hire and fire without a moment's thought and was not obliged to cater for their well-being. Their feelings about the matter were not very important, because the vast majority of those employed in these new industrial factories were providing physical labour with the minimum of skill or conscious thought required, rather like human pack-donkeys. The manager's job was not to take care of these workers' physical needs and far less to consider their emotional well-being, but to extract as much work from them as possible, while paying them as little as possible, and getting rid of any workers who were not up to the job. There being no health insurance or unemployment benefit in those days, if you could not cope with the heat, you ended up in the workhouse. The state and even social pillars like the church upheld this status quo and a belief that was commonly held at the time was that if workers were treated too well, they would become indolent and insolent. This was the era in which a hymn was written that included the words, "The rich man in his castle, the poor man at his gate. God made them high and lowly, each to his own estate." And that pretty much sums up the prevailing attitude of both society and management at the time: workers had been created by God to labour for their superiors.

Unsurprisingly, the life expectancy of the typical late-eighteenth or early nineteenth century factory worker was significantly less than that of the hunter-gatherer aeons before and we know from skeletal remains from both populations that their health was infinitely worse. Fortunately, the workers did not know this, and even if they had, they would have been too tired to worry about it.

By the mid-nineteenth century, large-scale shipping and railway freight had become possible thanks to innovations in transportation and mechanics. By the end of the nineteenth century, electricity was commonplace in industry and in urban homes. As Britain, in particular, grew ever wealthier, its empire continued to expand and so did its industries.

It was during the period of the industrial revolution that the first scholars of economics and management (as we can identify them in retrospect) began to look at issues of employee development and of helping employees to develop skills so as to make them more fully rounded human beings, while encouraging company growth. At the same time, the social conscience of the managing classes began to become a little bit more refined, as early pioneers in the area of rewarding good behaviour began to offer their workers such treats as minimal education for their children and—if they were lucky—a place to sit and eat their daily meal. However, understanding that the worker's access to education, training and acceptable working conditions were related to his productivity was an idea that had already been mooted and that, gradually, was gaining some acceptance.

As early as 1776, Adam Smith had written that personal earnings were closely related to whether or not the individual had had the opportunity to acquire an education or a set of skills. It took quite a while before the full impact of his observations began to enter the equation, but eventually the penny dropped: Workers who received training and/or education in their field were usually better workers. They were more involved with what they did. They had more opportunities to advance and, in the process, more to offer to their organisation.

The fifth age of management: reason enters the equation

It was not until the mid-nineteenth century that, in the context of a general flowering of economic, political and scientific thought, that a more carefully thought-out approach to management emerged, not to speak of the concept of "the worker"—or at least the trained, skilled worker—as a fully sensate human being who had practical, emotional and spiritual needs that were not entirely divorced from what happened in the workplace.

The style of management that we still use today was born in 1856, a date that *should* be engraved into the mind of every graduate of business studies but that is not, because we in the world of management tend to have our eyes focused on the here and now, forgetting about all that we can learn from the past.

1856 and the birth of scientific management

1856 was the year that the first organisation chart, that stalwart of management studies, was ever penned. That was the year that Daniel McCallum became the inventor of what he thought of as "function management", which was later developed as the Scientific Management that is still in use today.

Daniel McCallum was, on the face of it, a surprising candidate for the role. Born in Scotland to parents who emigrated to New York, he was a civil engineer by trade and, by 1855, was employed as a superintendent of the New York and Erie Railroad. Even by that time, the Railroad had become a very complex organisation, employing hundreds of workers at every level. McCallum looked at the business and realised that it was not performing at capacity; it took days to complete journeys that should have been possible to complete in hours. McCallum quickly pinpointed the reason why; there was simply no way that any one authority could maintain charge over such a vast, sprawling network, one that was growing even vaster and more complex all the time. In his own words, he said, "A superintendent of a road fifty miles in length can give its business his professional attention and may be constantly on the line engaged in the direction of its details; each person is personally known to him, and all questions in relation to its business are at once presented and acted upon; and any system however imperfect may under such circumstances prove comparatively successful [but] when one attempts to manage a railroad five hundred miles in length a very different state exists. Any system which might be applicable to the business and extent of a short road would be found entirely inadequate to the wants of a long one."

Given the fact that railroads were growing exponentially—on some lines at a rate of ten miles a day, thanks to the tireless efforts of the thousands of Chinese labourers who had been shipped in for the work—and that the extant lines were already an immense challenge to management, there was no way to improve the performance of the company as a whole; the only thing to be done was to break the railroad down into its various components and work on improving each one of those, one at a time.

McCallum started to apply his theory to his division, the New York to Chicago route, and managed to reduce journey time from three days to a matter of hours. Just think of how long that route is, and how many people must work on it. There is the rolling stock, the guardsmen, the employees working on the carriages, the station masters, maintenance staff, administrative staff, cleaners, engineers…the list goes on and on, and at the same time, new routes were constantly being built and industries springing up alongside them.

It seems obvious in retrospect, but Daniel McCallum's brainwave was to isolate each specific role within the railway system and manage it as a discrete unit rather than attempting to manage the whole complex organisation from the top. In other words, he had hit on the idea of dividing a company up into departments, with each department answerable on a daily level to its internal managers. Track maintenance staff would report to the head of track maintenance, cleaning staff would report to the head of cleaning, and so on. Top managers were freed to concentrate on larger issues, because the details of running the enterprise were being handled efficiently at a local level.

McCallum did not delay in instigating his new system. First, he broke the railroad down into manageable geographical divisions, and appointed a superintendent for each division. Each superintendent had to submit reports to headquarters, from where McCallum was able to control the general movements of the railway. Lines of authority were clear and easy to understand. McCallum was able to portray his new system as an ideogram, creating the first organisational chart.

With astonishing speed, railroads became the largest industrial organisations for their time. This in turn led not only to the dissemination of ideological influences, but also to the fact that, suddenly, it was much easier for industries to use railways to reach national markets and obtain supplies from far away. Many industries grew and, as they did, they followed McCallum in creating organisational divisions that oversaw production by means of what came to be known as "vertical integration".

Relatively quickly, this revolutionary approach started to gain favour and company heads began to hire people who would manage specific functions within the business, such as accounts, sales or production. For the first time, companies began to be run by professionals who were no longer simply funders or sycophants of the CEO but people who devoted themselves in a singular fashion to specific areas of the business and who had considerable authority and control over their division. The practical result for the consumer was, as we have seen, phenomenal and the basic format of company organisation has remained unchanged ever since.

Purely by coincidence, 1856 was also the year of the birth of the next great thinker in management, Frederick Taylor.

Like McCallum, Taylor was an engineer by trade. He was born into a wealthy Quaker family in Pennsylvania, but learned his trade through a combination of working on the shop floor at Midvale Steel Company and by following a correspondence course with an Institute of Technology (at the time, gaining a qualification by correspondence was itself a rather adventurous approach.) By the time he was twenty-two, Taylor was promoted to Gang Leader—pretty much what we would today refer to as Junior Manager. Taylor's approach to management showed his technical background. He became convinced that the way to optimise performance was to study each task in minute detail, break it into its component parts and time each component with a stop-watch, finally arriving at the average performance time for any given task. No task was too humble for Taylor's stopwatch. Once a norm had been set, there was a standard against which to judge the worker. Performing in less than the usual time meant that he was under-performing, while performing in more meant that he was over-performing. One of Taylor's first studies arrived at the conclusion that the ideal load for a shovel weighed two and a half pounds, and led him to find and design shovels that were perfectly adapted for carrying this precise weight for the given material. Yes, Taylor was nothing if not thorough!

Taylor was not impressed by the management practices he saw around him. So far as he could see, they led to time-wasting and, perhaps most importantly, did not reward workers for working well, giving them little incentive to work towards enhancing their performance. He believed that, if workers and management cooperated and applied scientific thought to the best way to do something, the result would be enhanced management and more efficient, cost-effective production. In his own words, he said, "Scientific management…has for its very foundation the firm conviction that the true interests of the two are one and the same; that prosperity for the employer cannot exist through a long term of years unless it is accompanied by prosperity for the employee, and vice versa; and that it is possible to give the workman what he most wants—high wages—and the employer what he wants—a low labor cost—for his manufactures."

The beauty of Taylor's approach was that he was speaking a language managers understood. He was talking about the bottom line. He did not suggest rewarding workers because they deserved it, or because it was the right thing to do. He pointed out that it made sense, because it was good for organisations. He was a scientist, through and through.

In 1911, Taylor's theories came to light as the book "Theories of Scientific Management," endorsing a five-step approach to Scientific Management:

❖ Studying and developing the best approach to any given task;

❖ Selecting the best worker to perform the task;

❖ Teaching and training the worker;

❖ Providing financial incentives to perform the task well;

❖ Dividing responsibility so that workers are responsible for working and managers responsible for planning.

Taylor introduced a number of concepts that were very controversial at the time, including rest breaks for workers so that fatigue did not hinder production. He also encountered resistance from company managers and owners who believed that permitting rest breaks would encourage workers to be indolent. Quite the opposite was true, and Taylor was prepared to prove it. In a case study, Taylor demonstrated that workers unloading ore performed better when they were given time during the day to rest; they were able to load *more* ore and to load it *faster,* even if they spent less actual time on the job, because their personal need for rest had been taken account of. Once again, Taylor was speaking to managers in a language they understood. Workers should not rest because they deserved to take a break but because they would work better if they did: "Practically all [heavy labour] consists of a heavy pull or a push on the man's arms, that is, the man's strength is exerted by either lifting or pushing something which he grasps in his hands. And the law is that for each given pull or push on the man's arms it is possible for the workman to be under load for only a definite percentage of the day. For example, when pig iron is being handled (each pig weighing 92 pounds), a first-class workman can only be under load 43 per cent of the day. He must be entirely free from load during 57 per cent of the day. And as the load becomes lighter, the percentage of the day under which the man can remain under load increases." What Taylor is suggesting here—that workers not work for 57% of the day so that they could work harder for the other 43%—was really revolutionary.

Taylor also noted that different people are suited for different jobs, and proposed that managers match each worker to a task suited to his particular talents and needs. In what would sound today like outright political incorrectness, he noted that more intelligent workers were not suited to employment that did not utilise their minds, while slow-witted people were ideally suited to simple physical tasks.

Taylor's approach quickly acquired disciples, and his methods were integrated into universities and industries all over the Western world in a surprisingly short period of time. In fact, Scientific Management is sometimes referred to as "Taylorism".

One of the European devotees of the approach was Frenchman, Henri Fayol. Having started at the mining company *Compagnie de Commentry-Fourchambeau-Decazeville*, Fayol gradually rose through the ranks until he was the Managing Director. In 1917, Fayol published *Administration Industrielle et Generale*, emphasising the importance of organisational structure in management. His book, which relies heavily on the ideas originally propagated by Taylor, was published in English in 1949 and Fayol is considered to be one of the major twentieth century thinkers in the area of management. Fayol identified what are now considered to be the four functions of management: planning, organising, leading and controlling. He stressed the importance of unity of command and direction, equity of treatment and team spirit, which he referred to as "*esprit de corps*". In Switzerland, American Edward Albert Filene established the International Management Institute to teach Scientific Management. Scientific Management had been accepted on just about every level as the only reasonable approach to managing the modern workplace.

Max Weber added bureaucratic theory to Scientific Management in his work that focused in hierarchy, authority and control and on the development of detailed standard operating procedures. Weber's most famous work, published in 1905, was *The Protestant Ethic and the Spirit of Capitalism*. He argued, among other things, that the reason why capitalism was more effective and more widespread in countries with a Protestant culture was because these cultures promoted an environment of working, saving and pride in one's work. However, his writing on the importance of bureaucracy to organisations sat well with the increasingly popular notion of Scientific Management. Weber drew a strong distinction between authority and power in organisations, using "power" to indicate when one person was able to impose his will over another, and "authority" to describe a situation whereby one person's will was seen as legitimate. "Rational legal authority" was the term he coined to describe how he felt management should take place, by observing a formal system of rules, valid within the organisation in question. Weber believed that if everybody within an organisation knew what the rules were and respected them as the best way to carry out interactions, leaders' authority would be acknowledged and respected and organisations could be run smoothly. One of the prerequisites of Weber-style bureaucracy was specialisation, or the division of labour. In other words, each organisation would have subunits devoted to specific tasks, such as sales or accounts. He also stressed the importance of remuneration, financial reward and promotions in recognition of good performance at work.

Mary Follett was born in Massachusetts in 1868, also into a well-to-do Quaker family, and became an important management and political theorist, much of whose work is still relevant today and many of whose contributions have been absorbed into Scientific Management, even though the vast majority of managers will never have heard her name. In fact, Follett's ideas about management still sound surprisingly modern; not for nothing has she been described as a "prophet of management". With a background in social work and studies of democracy, one of the key notions Follett brought to management was that of conflict resolution, incorporating the notion that differences in opinion and thought could be seen as opportunities for growth within organisations, as challenges rather than simply as problems. Her contribution to management theory was that power should be exercised *with* a company's employees rather than *over* them, and she espoused negotiation and resolution rather than power struggles whenever there was an apparent conflict of interest. In Boston, where she spent much of her adult life, Follett worked at establishing minimum wages and ongoing education for adults. However, while she was interested in organisations from the point of view of the rights of the workers within them, she was also a hard-nosed pragmatist who explored how organisations could handle the people within them to ensure the best possible outcome to work and team cooperation. In 1924, she published an important volume on management, Creative Experience, which focussed on team work, learning and innovation, and resonated with organisations that had adopted Scientific Management and believed in investing in their workforce. The following year, she presented a paper at the annual conference of the Bureau of Personnel Administration in New York, The Psychological Foundations of Business Administration, in which she argued that organisations could be viewed as communities or social systems containing networks of groups. By interacting with each other directly, she maintained, the various group members "fulfilled themselves through the process of the group's development".

With the growth in the United States of distrust in anything that sounded remotely socialist, Follett was less popular than in Britain, where a posthumous collection of her writings on management was published in 1941. Sadly, two of the biggest questions one can pose about Follett is, why have so few people heard of her and, more importantly, why have we failed to implement her suggestions more completely? Perhaps the answer lies in the fact that she was even further ahead of her time that at first seems. In her remark that the best leader, "knows how to make his followers actually feel power themselves, not merely acknowledge his power," and that leaders, "should lead by force of example. If those led obey the law of the situation, they must realize that he is doing the same. If they are to follow the invisible leader, the common purpose, so must he. If everyone must work overtime, the president should be willing to do the same. In every way he must show that he is doing what he urges upon others," we can begin to understand why.

The sixth age of management: ...and then everything started to change

By the 1920s and 30s, Scientific Management had been adopted all over the developed world. Surprisingly quickly, people stopped worrying about who had originally devised the ideas that they were now implementing and accepted Scientific Management as a sort of dogma. It was palpably better than any alternative that had been used to date and hard to imagine how it could be improved upon. In the main, the adoption of Scientific Management brought huge benefits to industry and, by and large, to workers, too. Management would probably never have got around to giving workers rest breaks because they deserved it, but when it was case of improving their output...well, that was a different story.

But society in this new century was changing quickly, more quickly than ever before and even more quickly than any of the nineteenth or early twentieth century thinkers on management organisation had envisioned. As Drucker remarked, "Throughout history, practically nobody had choices. Until about 1900, even in the most highly developed countries, the overwhelming majority followed their father's line of work—if they were lucky. If your father was a peasant farmer, you were a peasant farmer. If he was a craftsman, you were a craftsman. There was only downward mobility; there was no upward mobility." Now, everything had changed. Technologies developed at an astonishing pace. Air travel was introduced and more and more people acquired automobiles. Telephony became commonplace and, by the 1930s, most homes in the industrialised West had radios and thus access to more information about their world and their economies than before. Cinemas began showing newsreels, precursors to the news channels that are on offer twenty-four hours a day today. Books and newspapers became cheaper. Ever greater numbers of people, including girls, were finishing secondary school, and the reading and listening public had a more sophisticated understanding of their world and the questions in it. Greater numbers began to attend universities and other third level institutions, including people from demographics that had never accessed higher education before. Little by little, and especially after the Second World War, women began to enter the industrial work-force as more than just cleaners and menial workers. Many tasks that previously had been carried out by human workers were now done by machines. Physical strength was no longer an issue for most jobs, but academic and technical know-how increasingly were; something that had profound ramifications for the potential career development of women. Telephones and telegrams had made communication across distances infinitely easier, and the relative cost of these technologies had come down. There was no longer such a vast social and educational gap between managers and their employees as more and more people self-identified as middle-class, with corresponding tastes and aspirations and employees began to want more from the companies they worked for; more recognition, more rights, more potential to develop and grow.

Despite all these changes, approaches to management changed very little throughout this period. Scientific Management had become entrenched, even though there was some awareness, at least, that the approach was flawed when it came to directing and coordinating the efforts of what we now refer to as "knowledge workers", thanks to the work of Peter Drucker who, earlier, had been the first scholar to recognise the far-reaching importance of Follett's work.

Peter Drucker was born in 1909 in Vienna, Austria, and moved to the United States in 1937. In the post-war period, he noted and began to study a fascinating phenomenon: the growing numbers and importance of people whose role in the business of production was primarily intellectual, rather than physical. He observed that, more and more, there were employees who knew far more about what they were doing than their bosses did, something that is even more the case today than it was then. Drucker emphasised the importance of recognising and providing for the social as well as financial needs of these highly trained workers who were strong assets in any company and devised the "management by objectives" approach, according to which performance is measured against objectives, and rewarded accordingly, as opposed to the more straightforward approach applicable in industrial production. Drucker also determined that companies have three responsibilities, which he named as:

❖ Making a profit;

❖ satisfying employees and;

❖ being socially responsible.

Now *that* was a surprise. The notion that companies were responsible for satisfying employees was really a very revolutionary one at the time. Even the most daring management theorists to date had largely devoted themselves to talking about treating workers well in terms of conditions, pay, and incentive. The idea that employees had to be satisfied by their bosses was quite extraordinary. In fact, most managers today have still not fully assimilated this fact. Unfortunately, Drucker's message has never been properly taken on board, and has certainly not been absorbed into the Scientific Management paradigm that continues to prevail.

Change began to accelerate in the 1960s, 70s and 80s, as society underwent vast cultural and technological upheavals—women's role in the workplace grew enormously, men's role in the family underwent changes, too, faxes became commonplace, the computer began to become an important tool, and the numbers of people graduating from secondary school, university and other centres of learning continued to grow—and *still* Scientific Management held sway. Still, the idea that workers needed to be satisfied by their work was largely ignored.

In the 1990s, the Internet became a central tool, freeing many workers—at least in theory—from the imperative of being physically at work every day, and making it possible for companies to maintain divisions in different parts of a country, or even in many different countries, without any serious problems of communication at all. Social commentators began to predict that a majority of workers would start working from home. This is something that, in fact, has largely failed to materialise by the time of writing.

Throughout this period, and especially in the latter decades, perhaps the most extraordinary transformation of the workplace has been the replacement of production workers by knowledge workers at so many levels. When Scientific Management was coined, perhaps 5% of workers were highly trained professionals, while most provided brute labour. Now, from plumbers to secretaries, computer programmers to carpenters, the vast majority of employees in the developed world bring to their workplace not their physical strength, but specific skills that they have acquired only through education, training and application; skills and knowledge that, frequently, their managers do not share. A phenomenon that is increasingly common is the employee who works all day, but whose work is a complete mystery to the person who is supposed to be managing him, so specialised and diverse have his tasks become.

Despite all these manifold and continuing changes, we are applying a form of management that is no longer adapted to our social and corporate environments. We are still operating with a system that sees the employer as graciously bestowing the gift of work on his employees, rather than vice versa. Is it any wonder we are experiencing problems in the modern work-place?

Through it all, Scientific Management has maintained its stronghold. Peter Drucker died in 2005 and, right up to the end, he continued pointing out that our economy is now based on the efforts of knowledge workers. In 2001, he was quoted in The Economist as saying: "This new knowledge economy will rely heavily on knowledge workers...the most striking growth will be in 'knowledge technologists': computer technicians, software designers, analysts in clinical labs, manufacturing technologists, paralegals. ...They are not, as a rule, much better paid than traditional skilled workers, but they see themselves as 'professionals.' Just as unskilled manual workers in manufacturing were the dominant social and political force in the 20th century, knowledge technologists are likely to become the dominant social—and perhaps also political—force over the next decades."

The seventh age of management: what is that all about?

We have entered a new period, one in which we will have to work hard to implement what I refer to as the "seventh age of management". By this I do not mean that we have started to manage our business and our lives in a new way, but that it is high time that we did.

In other words, and with no disrespect to Taylor, Fayol, Follett, et al, it is now time to tear up the template and start over, because Scientific Management is just not cutting the mustard anymore. Production methods and systems of management that worked very well when largely untrained workers slaved over an assembly line are just not relevant today. What is worse, they are preventing us from being all that we could be, and affecting our quality of life, efficiency of work and company revenues negatively. Hence the Votive Process and this book, which makes a series of concrete, carefully researched proposals as to how we can devise and implement a thoroughly new, utterly reworked way of managing our businesses today; one that will change the way we work, live and interact immeasurably, and for the better.

Understanding knowledge workers

The term "knowledge worker" has been around since 1959, when Peter Drucker coined it in his book Landmarks of Tomorrow to describe people whose primary function in the workplace is using and developing knowledge. These workers are a primary asset of their companies, because not only do they know how to perform key tasks, but they are in a position, intellectually and educationally, to problem-solve and improve on their skill-set in a focused, targeted way, throughout their tenure with a given company. Given the right circumstances, they enjoy problem-solving and should be able to monitor their own progress through any given task. In the right environment, they are able to grow their skills incrementally, and continue to work creatively and well throughout their working lives.

The concept of knowledge workers came from a scholastic environment in which the notion of human capital was gaining acceptance; in other words, the understanding that human beings with all their innate and acquired capacities and skills represent a crucial element of the production function. In the same year, Mincer introduced the idea in his doctoral dissertation.

Hot on his heels were other scholars, including Becker and Schultz. The idea that it was worth investing in the training and development of one's employees gathered strength as the concept of individual talent as a vital element in production gained respectability.

The notion of people as assets in an organisation, who contribute hugely to its success and as entities that should be invested in is a good one, but it is limited insofar as it seems to take the "person" out of the "worker" and reduce the individual to a set of skills that can be used in the workplace.

We can consider as a "knowledge worker" anyone whose primary contribution to their workplace are the skills and specialised knowledge that they have acquired in the course of their education and working life, as opposed to physical strength or presence. In other words, the teenager flipping burgers is not functioning as a knowledge worker, but the trained secretary, accountant, sales representative or IT professional is.

Increasingly, corporations in the West and in other economies need academically qualified people working for them. At the time of writing, for example, knowledge workers outnumber all other North American workers by about four to one. This puts management in the peculiar situation of being, often, the least "expert" people in the organisation, as they are wholly dependent on being surrounded by experts, by knowledge workers, to get the job done.

How has this situation been created? On the one hand, a relatively high standard of education is now the norm for most citizens of the developed world—certainly, relative to the situation that prevailed one hundred years ago. On the other hand, more people are bringing to the workplace more specialised knowledge than ever before. What we have seen over the course of the past few generations has been the increasing specialisation of knowledge and work, until it has reached the point whereby many of us would not understand what half our colleagues are doing, even if they tried to explain it in the simplest vocabulary available. An IT specialist will have further sub-specialities that he is an expert in, but might not be familiar with—for example—every computer language that there is. An accountant might have a specialised skill set to deal with agricultural accounting, personal accounting or corporate accounting. While, in the past, the grunt-work was done on building sites by a large number of men using their hands and backs, much is now done by builders who have been trained in the operation and safety requirements of cranes and other machinery, and who will be specialised in fields such as bricklaying, plumbing or window fitting.

What manager has time to understand every single task that is being carried out in his company?

Of course, managing people whose roles in the organisation are not necessarily understood in detail poses a set of particular challenges. For example, Internet security is a pressing issue for most modern businesses. Somebody working in a small business or from a home office may be able to rely on an off-the-shelf security system, but a large company will need to hire someone, or even a whole team, to provide an in-company security service. This person or team will need to have a specialised understanding of computer networks, the Internet and how to protect computer systems from vulnerabilities. Even if the manager has a relatively high level of computer literacy, he is unlikely to know exactly what technician X does all day long. All that matters to him is that it…whatever it is…ensures that the company does not have any problems with computer security. How, then, is technician X supposed to be managed? How will he measure his achievements, or set goals?

It is a conundrum. What is more, it has been recognised as a conundrum for quite a while.

As we mentioned before, Peter Drucker pointed out that knowledge workers could not be managed in the same way as manual workers. Their way of working is different, their priorities are different, and their output is much more difficult to measure than that of the manual worker in a steel factory.

And yet, look at how companies are still being managed today. Almost exclusively, they are still applying management techniques that were devised in the nineteenth century in an utterly different industrial, social, and political environment. Why? There is no good reason for this degree of conservatism. We would look askance at the doctor who tried to cure us with nineteenth century medical know-how and few of us would travel from London to New York by steamboat to attend a business meeting.

Attempting to apply hard, metric measurements to determining whether or not knowledge workers are meeting their "objectives" is really no different. What was good, workable management practice in the context of nineteenth and early twentieth century businesses is no longer good, and it is no longer workable.

The result of our failure to devise a new approach to managing knowledge workers is that many knowledge workers are profoundly dissatisfied at work and, in consequence, are not working as well as they could and should, and are leaving workplaces with monotonous regularity. Today, all businesses recognise that retention of talent is a core fundamental challenge.

Variations on a theme

While all businesses have problems with management today, the situation is exacerbated by factors such as the size and complexity of the organisation. In a small company, members tend to multi-task. They develop closer relationships with each other, and are generally aware of the major life events of their colleagues, and of their strengths and challenges in the workplace. Because the organisation is not large, there is no problem of compartmentalisation, and because everybody knows each other, it is easier to tailor an approach to managing the work performance of each individual in the company.

However, as a company grows in size and complexity, so do the challenges facing managers. With more employees, there is the loss of a company-wide sense of community, and managers resort to our default model of management; the 1856 approach created by Daniel McCallum that is utterly unsuited to contemporary working culture. They resort to a very directive style, with a focus on accountancy and output, and forget about the human beings who are the organisation at its most fundamental. Typically, this is the stage at which many of the talented individuals who were originally the life-force of the company become dissatisfied and leave, because their professional, emotional, and psychological needs are no longer being met within the organisation.

Managers are keenly aware of the problem of tested, gifted individuals leaving organisations, and staff retention is a key issue for any large organisation. Most company managers will utter the words, "Our people are our most important asset." They may even believe them. But do they put their money where their mouth is? Absolutely not. When one explores where and how budgets are actually being spent, or looks at the budget allocated to IT, as opposed to development and training, the emphasis is generally on hard measurables such as scientific skills development, with an end goal of satisfying the company's accountant rather than on developing the worker—the human being—as an individual who will be fully realised within the company environment. We can refer to this as the "accountancy paradigm"; it is the balance book that matters, rather than the company's long term financial health. Companies behave as if society had not changed, but just think about all the revolutionary shifts that have occurred in just the past few decades. More people are working from home, part- or full-time, and this is a trend that will only continue. Because of our changing roles in society, both women and men are juggling family and work commitments, and are increasingly no longer prepared to work long hours every day, and return home after their children have gone to bed. People job share, take career breaks, telecommute, work freelance or operate a combination of the above. The "job for life" is largely a thing of the past. The beloved organisational chart has become incredibly complex. Thanks to the technologies we now employ, our companies can be spread all over the place. HR and accounting do not need to be anywhere near head office anymore. Let's move accounting to Mumbai and HR to Leeds; why ever not?

What is interesting is that, despite the vast changes that we are still undergoing, our emotional needs as living, breathing human beings have not changed in the least. They are just more difficult to meet. More and more of us knowledge workers rarely physically meet our colleagues, let alone our managers. We acquire skills and put them to use in an increasingly lonely work environment. We can do much more than we could before; how many of us use a typist to write our emails? How many of us can make our PowerPoint© presentations for ourselves? Despite the awkward management systems that are being used, we are more productive than ever before, but we are also less content within the corporate environment—and that makes it harder for our managers to keep us, as we shift restlessly from one company to the next, looking for the emotional and psychological fulfilment that perennially prove to be so elusive. Our organisations think that they are offering us the chance to grow by sending us on one-off courses to hone our computer skills, or teach us a new program or accounting technique. They overlook the fact that we are actually very good at acquiring new skills. Where we really need help is in the area of developing new ways of looking at what we do, and interacting with our managers, our employees and our colleagues, and new beliefs about what we do, how we do it and why we do it. This will mean that money and time—but especially time—will have to be spent on developing attitudes and the "soft" human skills of interaction, communication and empathy.

In my role as consultant, I ask every group I work with about the challenges that they are facing with respect to work issues in the company. Some common themes invariably emerge: answering the floods of emails that arrive every day, hitting profits, coping with the workload, keeping customers and maintaining an acceptable work/life balance for all the company's employees.

"If someone was to be hired tomorrow," I ask. "What sort of person would they need to be?"

Again, the answers tend to be pretty consistent. The new employee would, I am informed, need to be focused, motivated, a good team player, driven, calm under pressure, blessed with a sense of humour, caring and sharing, willing to work, and prepared and able to be creative. What is more, managers and employees alike present the same list of core attributes. There is an astonishing degree of consistence, regardless of the sort of business the organisation is in.

Examining the ideal attributes listed above, it is easy to see that they refer to qualities that are a mixture of skill and attitude. Again, there is a lot of consensus as to which element is more important; the balance always lies towards attitude, about 80/20 or 70/30. Skills are relatively easy to acquire, given a base level of intelligence and access to education or training. The right *attitude* is the facilitator that makes all the difference. The right attitude makes it possible for one to access one's ability and skills and implement them in the right way, in the right place, and at the right time.

Why, if management and employees all recognise that attitude is, on balance, even more important than skills, do businesses today invest so little time, energy, and money in developing attitude, and in creating the sort of workplace where healthy attitudes flourish and the company benefits as a result? The fact is that most of them have not yet woken up to the fact that Scientific Management is a largely obsolete way of doing things for a compound of reasons that we will be discussing as we continue with this book.

Knowledge workers work better and produce more when they are given the power and authority they need to make the most of their skills; when the company's environment fosters a situation within which "soft" factors, such as emotional intelligence, can be used to maximise the outcome of their effort.

But how closely do the typical company's actions match their words? Let's see.

Typically, the vast bulk of the training budget is spent on skills—studying that new computer program, learning that new sales fad—and pennies on attitude. Why, when everyone agrees that attitude is what makes the business? Of course, skills are important. The 20% skill element that goes into making the ideal worker is crucial. But having skills and knowing, in theory, how to use them, just does not necessarily translate to good performance. When it comes to turning those skills into results, attitude is what makes all the difference. It does not make any difference whether you work in a public or private business, whether you are left- or right-brain oriented, or indeed whether you work in a sports kit or a suit and tie. If you are not motivated to put your skills to good, intelligent use, they are about as helpful as a third nipple.

Today's knowledge workers live and work in an environment where attitude matters more than ever before. Human-to-human interactions, whether in person, by email, by phone, or whatever, are essential. Individual workers are carrying out more analyses by themselves. They are applying their knowledge to whatever they do, whether it is selling televisions on the shop floor or pitching for a multi-million pound contract for a blue chip organisation.

And how do they feel about it?

The sad fact is that our persistent use of Scientific Management is letting all these people down. Too many workers feel as though they are being managed as if they were hamsters on a wheel, running and running and running, and never really getting anywhere. Restless and frustrated, they leave one organisation for another, only to find themselves running fruitlessly around on yet another wheel. Nor is the situation much better for their managers, who are trying to motivate and keep knowledge workers, all the while using a framework that was created as long ago as 1856, and hardly modified at all in the intervening years.

So, let's welcome the Seventh Age of Management!

Let's look at our priorities, and decide to make them the focus of the way we live, work and manage.

Let's start over.

Chapter 2)
The Customer Service Tsunami

Anytime a customer comes into contact with any aspect of a business,
however remote, is an opportunity to form an impression—Jan Carlzon

O ver the course of the last twenty years or so, we have seen a change in notions about and expectations of customer service that can only be described as a "tsunami", for its speed and its radical nature. This change has swept across the Western world, altering the expectations of both workers and customers in very profound ways, changing the workplace and the customer/worker interface profoundly, and transforming our expectations in terms of life-style and accountability immeasurably.

At its most simple, we see the effects of this tsunami in the fact that companies today are much more customer-oriented than they used to be. One of the reasons for this is the simple fact that customers are very much more discerning than before. They know that there are many ways to get what they want, and they are unlikely to stick with a company that gives them bad service or shoddy products. If they cannot find what they want in a shop or office near their home, they can probably find an alternative product on the Internet, or order it on the phone. This degree of flexibility, from the consumer's viewpoint, means that every company's job today is to keep the customers that they already have, increase the debt that they have with them, and work on increasing their share of the customer market by attracting new customers. Given all the competition, the only way to do this is to maintain an extremely customer-focused approach in every aspect of the business. Many companies offer very similar products or services, and it is not always easy to differentiate qualitatively between these products and services; what is better, a book from Waterstones or the same one from W.H. Smith? A Big Mac or a Whopper? MasterCard or Visa? A night at the local Hilton or a night at the local Best Western? And yet, customers' experiences of identical or near-identical products or services can be very different, depending on their interaction with the product or service provider. They will return to the shop or restaurant or hotel where they felt cared about as individuals, where their opinions and tastes were taken seriously. Where customer service was palpably central to the organisation's modus operandi. Yes, the difference in terms of customer satisfaction often lies in customers' experience of interacting with the company in question. An example? You have almost certainly heard of Internet retail giant Amazon. Initially launched in 1997 to sell books, Amazon quickly diversified to provide a wide range of consumer goods via the Internet, including entertainment paraphernalia and equipment, clothes, and household goods. The company's experience has not all been plain sailing—negotiating the new retail environment of the Internet was a steep learning curve for anyone who dared to go there in the 1990s—but despite ups and downs, Amazon has weathered the storms and consistently performed better than its nearest competitors, such as Barnes and Noble, as well as a myriad of smaller companies, most of which went belly-up. The reason why? Well, in November, 2006, MarketWatch identified Amazon as the winner in a United States nation-wide survey of the companies with the best customer service. Although customers rarely, if ever, interact directly with Amazon employees, the consumer/retailer interface is focussed on the consumer not just as the bearer of the all-important credit card, but as a human being whose needs are respected, and whose individuality is recognised. The company utilises software that uses customer's previous choices to suggest other items that they might like to buy, on the basis of their preferences. It is easy to contribute directly to the site in the form of a review, and Amazon customers become not just shoppers, but also part of a virtual community of sorts. They feel involved with the company, and when their reviews are posted, they can see that their views are respected, and their experience with Amazon is not one of being treated as a mere number, but as someone who matters; all of this without so much as ever seeing one single Amazon employee! MarketWatch quoted the United States National Retailers Federation President, Tracy Mullin, as saying that, "Consumers are beginning to demand more from retailers and are making conscious decisions about where to shop based on their expectations for good service."

Quite.

Conversely, look what happened when IBM failed to take note of the huge cultural changes occurring around us, and just did not change with the times. IBM once dominated the field of computation to the extent that any other organisation in computers was brushed off like a Jack Russell nipping at the heels of an Alsatian. Then, as so often happens, IBM grew arrogant. It was used to being the only big player in the field, and it made little effort to make computers accessible to the masses, or to communicate effectively with its customer base. In 1993, IBM's Lou Gerstner famously announced, "The last thing IBM needs right now is a vision."

Then, along came companies like Microsoft and Apple—companies that were all about making computers easier to use, cheaper to purchase, and more relevant to the life experiences of ordinary people; companies whose very modus operandi was based on what the customer wanted and expected. There were help centres, training manuals, customer-friendly interfaces, and products that people wanted and were able to purchase and use. The rest, of course, is history. How many of us work with Microsoft products or use an Apple computer? How many of us have stuck with IBM? IBM quickly lost 50% of its revenue from sales of its main product lines and almost went belly-up. Over the course of the years to come, IBM had to realise that yes, they did need to have a vision, and that that vision had to incorporate generous allocations of time and effort to keeping customers happy. At the time of writing, IBM is a more successful organisation than it has been in recent years, but it is still very, very far from coming close to approaching the success enjoyed by Microsoft.

Banking on the future

One industry where the effects of the customer service tsunami can be seen very clearly is banking, the area that I first worked in after ten years in the Army. Banking, of course, originally developed as a service for the wealthy—the elite—and not for Joe Average. This showed, long after Joe Average had signed up for an account. Indeed, when I first joined the world of banking, in the 1980s, the manager was still almost like a small deity;

above everyone else and almost unapproachable. We used to joke that he would come in in the morning, and that minions would fall into place in front of him, tossing rose petals before him as he walked. Like all good jokes, this was funny because there was more than a modicum of truth in it. In those days, the typical manager would say "good morning," in a casual manner to the people he passed as he made his way to his lavishly-appointed office. Once ensconced, he would drink some tea, sign a few papers and then leave for a long, boozy lunch at the local Rotary Club. In the afternoon, he would pop back into the office with a hint of whisky on his breath, sign a few more papers, and then disappear home.

Nice work if you can get it, right?

Of course, this was also in the days when banks opened between 9.30 in the morning and 3.30 in the afternoon and closed for lunch; hardly the most customer-friendly environment imaginable. Working practice in the bank seemed to have been designed for the comfort and convenience of the managers, and it probably was. But because there was no real option, the customer had to take it or leave it. Think of the person living and working in an ordinary market town in the United Kingdom in the 1970s. Maybe there were three or four banks, so you chose the one that seemed to offer you the most, or the one in which the managers and assistants were the friendliest, and then arranged your working life so that you could go to the bank when you needed to. If you wanted a loan, you had to take time off work to see someone at the bank, and then grovel and beg while they questioned your ability to repay it, until you felt as though they were giving your three piece suit the once-over, and deciding that it had seen better days. That was just the way things were. It was the way things had *always* been, it seemed. Certainly, few people had any idea of just how dramatically things were about to change.

In today's banks, everything is different. Nowadays, banks are run as retail environments, and frequently headed by managers who are as young as twenty-four or twenty-five. The staff behind the counter are no longer just service providers; they have become retail assistants, and it is now their job to try to sell you as much as they possibly can—loans, a new pension fund, a savings account for those rainy days...

The days of going into the bank and grovelling for a loan are long over. Now, the banks are desperate for you to come in and ask for a loan. In fact, they are desperate for you to come into the bank at *all*. If anyone is grovelling and begging, it is the banks, with their special offers here and their special offers there, their free Internet banking and constant innovations designed to make the banking experience easier and less stressful for the consumer. Now banks have to go out and hustle for business with online offers, direct mailing, cold calling, and all the rest of it. Most of all, they have to treat their customers really, really well if they want to hold onto them.

Where has this change come from? The biggest factor has got to be that customer expectations have changed enormously, partly because of shifts in society, but mostly because of the differences in customer service that have been made possible by technologies that have utterly transformed the way we interact with retail and service environments, and that have done away with the notion that one has to bank in the best option available in one's immediate geographical area. Today's bank customers expect to be able to do their banking twenty-four hours a day; no more having to find time out of a busy work day to go to the bank. They want to do their banking by phone, and they expect to be able to do it on their computer. They want to be able to move money from London or Dubai to Hong Kong, and they want and expect to be able to access the same service everywhere they go. They are asking for a lot, and if their bank cannot or will not give it to them—well, they will simply move their custom elsewhere, because there are other banks that will. In the developed world, we are blessed in having almost unlimited access to information, products and services. Cannot find the book you are looking for at Waterstones? No problem—you can get it shipped over from Chicago, and it might even cost less, too. What is more, you will save yourself the trip into town in the process.

Where did it all come from?

To the consumer, the modern world seems to be a much smaller, more approachable place than it used to. At the same time, we are being educated every day by the multiple strands of the media as to how much more we can have; how much better we can be served, and what we could and should be aspiring to. Twenty years ago, the average Briton would not have known where Kazakhstan and Afghanistan were. Now, images and news from these far-away places are brought straight into our homes by cable news channels, real-time Internet, and more traditional media, such as newspapers. It is relentless. It is 24/7. It makes even the far-away and the exotic seem as though they are right next door. And it is as much a part of the world we now live in as is the very air we breathe.

Let's look at just one example: Ireland. Twenty-five years ago, Ireland was a second world country. The best and brightest of the young university graduates left the country. Poverty—real poverty—was a serious problem. Many people were still in farming, at a time when small-scale agriculture was, increasingly, no longer a viable way to maintain an acceptable lifestyle. Now, Ireland has one of the healthiest economies around, attracting workers and investors from all over the world, including countries to which Irish people once flocked for work. What happened? Various elements colluded to create the booming economy that has been making the headlines for the past ten years. For a start, following Ireland's accession into the European Union in 1973, the Union (or the European Economic Community, as it was then known) invested a lot of money in what was then an astonishingly underdeveloped island nation and, on balance, it was spent well, on developing technology and funding education. Now, Ireland is not just a dynamic community, but an important centre for industry and commerce in Europe. For America, Ireland is the English-speaking stepping stone to the European market. Every major blue-chip organisation has a representative there. They cannot afford not to, because Ireland has become a central hub. When search engine giant Google decided to set up in Europe, Ireland was the obvious choice. Whereas, in the past, Ireland exported doctors and engineers, nurses and labourers, now it has immigration to the extent that 10% of the population is not of Irish descent, up from a statistically insignificant minority much less than a generation ago. Mandarin is now the country's second most widely-spoken language, beating even the indigenous Gaelic tongue. Materially, the population is well-off. Property and other tangible assets are worth sums that would have been unthinkable only recently, and the young people who are growing up and joining the workforce are starting out from a basis of wealth and prosperity. From being an island on the fringes of Europe, backward, old-fashioned, superstitious and corrupt, Ireland has become an integral part of the modern global economy. The true answer as to why lies with access to information, which has effectively nullified Ireland's island status. Ireland's current success owes a great deal to the customer service tsunami.

Everywhere in the developed world, alongside this information comes material that is forming us as a new type of consumer; information about items we did not even know we wanted until we had heard of them, information about new ways to shop and new ways to pay. Information about places we did not know existed, but that we are now being exhorted to visit. Every day, we are learning more about how much more we want.

The consequence is a generation that has more drive and ambition than any generation that preceded it.

Of course, it is not all plain sailing. We are in a period of transition right now, and there are some bumps along the way. Partly because our expectations vis a vis lifestyle have changed so radically—the average family now takes foreign holidays and exotic tastes at the table for granted—most do not feel able to sustain their household on just one income, or even on one and a half. Married couples with children tend to feel under constant pressure, as they struggle to maintain an adequate life/work balance, with Mum and Dad both arriving home late, exhausted from their day. Grandparents are living longer and healthier, and their expectations as consumers and citizens of this new world have changed too; Granny is less likely to be at home baking scones and taking care of the little ones, than spending the winter in the south of Spain, trekking in Nepal, or floating her new start-up on the stock market.

Even adults who are now just in their late 20s and early 30s can look back at all the changes that have taken place in the world, and feel dizzy at the scope and extent of how different things are. We are living in the future. It is marvellous and it is awful, and it is where we are. We have got to deal with it, and with our era's multiple challenges and opportunities.

However, despite all these massive cultural changes—"revolution" is certainly not too strong a word here—*we are still applying 1856 management styles*. We are trying, with increasing desperation, to make them work in a society in which everything else has changed.

Well, I have got news for you. It is time to stop. We have got to do more than update and reform. We have got to simply change our fundamental approach to notions of authority and answerability. We have got to change the very nature of management itself. We have got to realise that the employee is a customer of his or her managers just as the account holder is a customer of the bank. The 1856 management style is bankrupt.

A new way of seeing employees

Most of us working in organisations that offer products or services are aware of the changes in customer service that have been rolled out in recent decades. Less obvious is the internal revolution in customer service that is still underway, and that is part of the wider revolution that is the dawn of the age of the knowledge worker.

Let me give a little example. A young woman I know, who is just about to sit her A-levels, attended an interview for a sixth-form college. Like many of her generation, having grown up in an era in which knowledge and skills are increasingly the only key to a bright future, she is a bright, get-up-and-go individual, who has far-reaching ambitions for her future. She is far more discerning and demanding than a seventeen-year-old of a previous generation would have been. At seventeen, she is already working hard to secure the sort of life that she would like to have.

"So," the head of the sixth form said in the interview, "do you know what you want to do when you leave school? Do you know who you want to work for?"

"Actually," the young woman said, "I don't want to work for anyone. I want to work for myself."

"So you want to be self-employed?"

"Not necessarily...actually, what I meant was that I expect to have a pretty good idea of where I want to go, and in a way *I* will be employing *them* to get to where that is. I don't want to work for someone for forty years, unless they are taking me to where I want to go."

This young woman has realised something that all senior managers would do well to understand; nowadays, the gift of employment is with the employee, not the employer. This, of course, is completely at odds with 1856 management styles. In the past, employees were expected to be grateful that they had a job. Seen as customers, however, everything changes. Just as the shop owner is happy and grateful when someone walks into his shop, so should the manager be happy and grateful when a gifted, talented individual brings those gifts and talents to the workplace. They need to look after their needs, and make sure that their experience of the organisation is all they hoped for. The viewpoint needs to be, "What can I do to make you feel better?"

For companies to be successful in not just pleasing customers but in retaining and cherishing valued employees, we need to start seeing management in terms of satisfying customers; the knowledge workers who bring their talent and expertise to the organisations they work for. But how do we recognise internal customers? It is very simple. Anyone working within an organisation, and sometimes depends on another member of that organisation, is an internal customer. The IT technician who needs to be told what he is expected to do; the junior manager who is asked to integrate a new process; the bookkeeper in charge of payroll who depends on each department supplying them with the relevant information every week. Applying customer service values to an organisation starts inside the organisation, not on the shop floor, the business website, or where external customers and staff interact. When customer service values prevail internally, they will create an atmosphere in which the external customer is also always a priority, and everybody will be completely tuned in to the importance of giving each moment of truth all they have got.

The term "moments of truth" was coined by Jan Carlzon, the former president of Scandinavian Airlines. He used this phrase to describe any interaction with a customer, each being an opportunity to provide a good experience and association with the organisation. In his business, these "moments of truth" were as simple as the smile on the face of the person at check-in, and courteous behavior on the part of stewards. What we are just beginning to learn today, is that we have just as many "moments of truth" within any given organisation, and each and every interaction we have with our colleagues and employees is a moment in which we are being offered the opportunity to promote an atmosphere of customer service within the company. Just as organisations that treat their external customers will do a better job of retaining their interest, so do organisations that treat their internal customers from a service perspective retain valued employees, and minimise the cost and disruption that ensue every time somebody has to be replaced.

From my own experience, I can cite an example of old-style management that really was not working out in an environment in which customer expectations had changed radically. Again, my example comes from Ireland.

A few years ago, I was employed to provide a consultancy service to Dublin Bus. As the name suggests, this is a transport system in Ireland's capital, providing a bus service within the city, and to commuters travelling from the suburbs to school and work. Since its inception in 1987 as a division of Ireland's nation-wide transportation system, Dublin Bus had been a semi-state body, heavily subsidised by the government. Dublin's bus transport system had long been notorious for its unreliability, lack of punctuality, impolite employees, and general lack of concern for its users, especially anyone who needed a little extra help, such as the elderly, parents with small children, and the disabled. Complaining about the city's bus service was part of Dublin culture. For years, since long before the transport system was reinvented as Dublin Bus, consumers had been unhappy about the transport available to them, much as anyone living at the same latitude as Ireland is unhappy about the long, grey winters. It was not good and everyone knew it, but at the same time it seemed to be as immutable as the weather.

When I arrived, I found managers who knew that they were letting their external customers down. They were aware that they would have to work on educating the drivers to see customers as people whose needs and requirements had to be respected in a courteous manner. They were aware that they had many improvements to make in the areas of punctuality and reliability, and they certainly knew that they had a lot to do in the area of improving their image in the city. When I talked to the drivers, I could see for myself the attitudinal problems that the managers were dealing with. Used to being public employees, the drivers said things like, "An empty bus is a happy bus," and stressed that they preferred to drive buses around a route with as few passengers as possible.

What was less obvious but just as damaging to the company was the fact that the drivers' emotional and practical needs, above and beyond relatively simple issues of pay and entitlements, were not being taken care of. Managers were aware that drivers had to change the way they worked. What they did not realise was that they, too, had to change the way they managed, and they had to stop seeing drivers as a problem, but as human beings whose emotional needs had to be met within the workplace, in order for them to become able to offer the service their consumers required. In other words, just as the drivers would have to work on developing a more highly evolved attitude towards their customers, the managers had to realise that, in turn, the drivers were *their* customers. They also had to accept that, in terms of customer service, they had been selling the drivers short. In fact, they had been giving them very shoddy service indeed. For example, one of the drivers whom I met had been the victim of a very unpleasant, if not dangerous, assault in which a mentally unstable member of the public had thrown urine on him. He had not been hurt, but had been extremely upset by the incident. When he went to the manager, he was told that he should just get over it, because it really was not a big deal. The manager completely overlooked the fact that bus drivers everywhere are painfully aware that, while most routes are safe, they also have to provide a transport service into and out of some of the city's most dodgy neighbourhoods. On any given day, the risk of a serious assault is minimal, but it is real, and all the drivers know it. This attack had tapped into the driver's fears of the worst that could happen. His anxiety was real, it was deeply felt, and it should have been respected. By dismissing his fears, his manager had seriously let him down as a customer within the work environment. How would you feel, if your experience as an external customer fell far short of the ideal, and you were told to "just get over it"? Internal customers deserve the same respect as external ones. By behaving in this way, of course, the manager was doing no more or less than simply following the established protocol of Scientific Management, seeing the worker as a mere cog in the wheel of the company's business, rather than a full human being, with all the strengths and weaknesses involved.

But it is not enough to point out that old styles of management are not working in the modern workplace, and to give examples from the many thousands of cases that present themselves. We have to understand *why*.

To find a management style in tune with the way we live today, it helps to see the worker within an organisation as not just an employee, but also as a customer. While we, as external consumers, want and expect utterly different things than before, internal consumers also want and expect very different things. In the outside world, we are no longer stoic about bad service in a restaurant; we are much more likely to complain. We feel that we deserve to get what we pay for. In the example I cited above, Dubliners had become fed up with the notion that their city's bus system could do whatever it wanted. They were paying for it, directly and through taxation, and they wanted to get what they were paying for. At the same time, drivers for Dublin Bus felt that they were being asked to providing a service day in, day out, without recognition and support from their managers. Similarly, within the companies and organisations we work for, we are all much unhappier about being told what to do, without explanation, without being asked for input, and without the emotional and practical support we know we deserve. Being treated this way is annoying, it is belittling, and it is not conducive to a good attitude to work. If our manager gives us a poor service in terms of helping us to realise our goals and providing back-up and support, we think, "This is no good. I am important. I am essential to the company's success. Why are not they letting me in on anything? Why are my opinions and feedback consistently ignored?"

If our opinions and feedback continue to be ignored, we will leave the company, or we will decide that, as it does not make any difference anyway, we will do the bare minimum we need to do, to avoid getting fired.

Some time ago, I was doing some work for Cadbury's. Cadbury's has a huge sales force, and one division's role is for its staff to go into all the shops that sell Cadbury's products, and work with what is known in the industry as a "Plannogram". A Plannogram is the retail display on which all the products are held. Now, there is a particular way of setting up the Plannogram that maximises the sale of certain types of chocolate over others. If Cadburys wants a run on one type of bar instead of other brands, they know how to set up the Plannogram in such a way that it will be sold in greater numbers.

The problem for Cadbury's is that the shop owners, and representatives from other chocolate manufacturers, come along and use the Plannogram to display other wares. The sales people have to visit the shops and rearrange the confectionary constantly. On the face of it, this might not seem like a highly skilled job, but knowledge work it certainly is, as it calls for considerable human skills in communicating well with shop owners and in maintaining motivation in the face of what is very repetitive work, day in, day out. Developing a good relationship with retailers is a key aspect of the salesperson's role, and their attitude is central to achieving this. At the time when I was called in, one of the main problems Cadbury's was experiencing was a very high attrition rate within the sales force. The work was monotonous in the extreme, and it was difficult to maintain morale in face of the difficulties involved in building relationships with the people in the retail environment. Our programme was designed to take management and help them to talk to their employees more, to work more with attitudinal issues, and to take more responsibility in understanding that the success of the sales team was ultimately *their* responsibility. As a result of learning how to recognise the customer needs of the sales team, retention of these key workers improved significantly.

A major distillery firm and spirits distributor facing a similar problem ran a programme for both employees and managers, one that tapped into not just their work, but their life skills and life needs, investing in workers as human beings. The programme focussed on how to make employees feel better on a daily basis, and showed them techniques that they could use to foster their own sense of happiness and job satisfaction through taking greater responsibility and accountability, and by moving away from blaming others when things went wrong to setting themselves goals, and then working to reach them. This investment in people as human beings, rather than as people who have to just "do stuff", helped them to achieve better relationships with their clients, just as Taylor's iron workers were able to work better and work harder when they were recognised as people who needed to take a break every now and again.

The reason why a customer service approach has not yet been fully integrated into the modern workplace lies in the fact that a new culture of training has not yet completely evolved. Managers know that there are problems with the way that most businesses currently do things, but they are not confident enough to bring in the sweeping changes that really are necessary.

We already know that most training does not work in terms of bringing tangible benefits to the workplace, and to the way in which managers and employees interact. In general, it does not create development, especially when you are talking about attitude and beliefs and motivational matters; the inner game stuff. For example, in an organisation in which I once worked, management talked about a lot of good ideas, and came up with great insights, but when it came to their attempts to implement them, the typical intervention was a one- or two-day programme; not something that would actually create long-term, beneficial change. After the programme, everyone would walk out feeling great—motivated, inspired and energetic. The problem was that in the absence of real lasting change, it did not take long for everyone to revert back to the old way of doing things. Because there was no real commitment to long-term application of the messages management was trying to get across, and minimal financial and emotional investment in following through with the lessons being taught, there was no substantive, long-term attitudinal change.

What is the problem? Basically, the problem lies in the fact that training organisations, just like all other organisations, have failed to develop a new approach. They tend to remain stuck with the view of training as a way of increasing employees' and managers' skill sets, rather than working on their underlying attitudes and feelings. The trend is that one goes on a course, after which Human Resources ticks a box and thinks, "OK, so that's it for skills development for this year! I have just put fifty people through a training program, so my job here is done." The fact that the same course will be taught the next year, with the same outcome—or lack of outcome—is not seen as what it is; indicative of a failure to make meaningful change.

In order to create a true atmosphere customer service, one has to get away from an accountancy paradigm, and be prepared to engage directly with the individual—to work towards a development paradigm, instead. Managers have to start spending time with people, treating the organisation more like an educational establishment, or a business to which employees have come as customers, as people who will not be able to fulfil their side of the bargain, unless their needs are catered to within a service environment.

It is not difficult to understand why this fails to create a culture of customer service within the workplace.

Moving away from Scientific Management

The problem lies with the fact that we are still using Scientific Management, despite the customer service tsunami that continues to reshape the retail, service and work environments, and form new types of opinions and expectations. Managers typically turn around and say, "I want you do better so that the company has more money coming in. You are going to have to work better and you are going to have to work harder."

Why does that not help? Well, unless the employee, the knowledge worker, is engaged with management and emotionally invested in the company, he is going to nod and say that he will work harder, but he does not really care. The company does not have enough money? No more big bonuses for the managers? Well, whatever. He has got a job to do, but unless it is a very small organisation and everyone is invested in the business, there is no reason for him to have developed any passion for the business at all. In fact, as soon as he hears that the company is not doing so well, he is more likely to think that it might be time to jump ship and find another work environment; one in which he is more secure and more likely to be able to develop as he would like to.

Scientific Management does not help to foster an environment in which knowledge workers care about the fate of the organisation in which they are working; it does not help them to become all they can be within the context of the organisation and, just like the customer who stops shopping at Acme Stores because of a bad experience, the knowledge worker will starting looking for a better job, a better experience with another company that he hopes will better fulfil his emotional and business needs.

The problem we have in management is exactly the same. Because we do not learn management in an adequate fashion—we do not study and learn from the past as we do in other areas—we end up with the exact same dogma being handed down from one generation to the next. "This is the way you manage," we are told. We are given facts and occasionally new ideas, but because the new ideas are not attached to a fundamental change in the way we think about management, because managers have not taken on board the fact that knowledge workers are their clients in the context of massive changes in customer expectations, it tends to disintegrate and fall apart.

Let's have a quick run-through some of the management fads that have emerged in the course of the past fifteen years. We have seen:

- ❖ Corporate Planning;

- ❖ Management by Objectives;

- ❖ SWOT analysis;

- ❖ Hierarchy of Needs;

- ❖ Hertzberg's Motivators and Maintenance Factors;

- ❖ Participant Management;

- ❖ Strategic Planning;

- ❖ Strategic Business;

- ❖ Portfolio Management;

- ❖ Quality of Life programs;

- ❖ Total Quality Management;

- ❖ The Excellence Syndrome;

- ❖ Self-directed Work Teams;

- ❖ Reengineering;

- ❖ The Learning Organisation;

- ❖ The Balanced Score-card;

- ❖ Benchmarking;

- ❖ Core Competences;

- ❖ Activity-based Costing;

- ❖ Value-chain Analysis;

- ❖ Variable-based Pay;

- ❖ Customer Relationship Management;

- ❖ Global Sourcing;

- ❖ Stakeholder Analysis;

- ❖ Economic Value Added;

- ❖ Six-sigma;

- ❖ Results management;

- ❖ Lean manufacturing.

Wow! That is a lot.

Now, all of these were great ideas in their various ways, but the problem is that even if a company tries to integrate a new approach to management, *it will not stick unless the basic format of management changes*. Typically, when an organisation tries to implement a new way of doing things, some changes will be made, they will work for a little while and then, gradually, old-style management will reign once more. The problem is that we are trying to apply these things within the framework of Scientific Management, and it just will not work.

What we really need is a new paradigm; a completely new way for thinking about working and living and providing an optimum service to our customers, external and internal alike. We have got to interact and work with staff in a very different way than before, setting aside archaic notions of hierarchy and duty. We have to move towards a much more holistic approach, which will release much more potential. When potential is unleashed, productivity can be improved through engaging with knowledge workers, through fulfilling their multiple needs as consumers. If you can improve productivity, you have got yourself a much better organisation. Feeling looked after themselves, the people within the organisation will look after it in turn. The bottom line is that it is the duty of managers to change first, because their new set of attitudes, and their new behaviours with relation to their employees, will create a positive atmosphere of customer service within the organisation; one that will change the way everybody works, interacts and lives in a very dramatic way. As soon as we stop seeing the people who work for us as mere "employees," with the almost negative connotations that have come to be associated with that word as a label, we can move beyond unhelpful notions of hierarchy. We can forge new mentalities, in which we see our employees as customers whose requirements need to be filled.

So, we know what knowledge workers are, and we know that we seriously need to reform the shape of the modern workplace to cater for their needs. But what are those needs, and how can they be met? Let's see, shall we?

PART TWO:

THE WAY WE SHOULD BE

Chapter 3)

Overcoming resistance, embracing risk and acquiring new habits

I am not the first to have pointed out that there is a problem with the way we manage our businesses today. The hundreds of management fads that consistently emerge with all the reliability of Christmas and Easter are testimony to the fact that most of us *do* realise that there is something very wrong indeed with the way we are going about things, and that we know it even as we resist—practically kicking and screaming—any real attempt to change it.

Dissatisfaction in the workplace is rife, even in booming economies, and workers and managers alike tend to be restless, endlessly moving from one organisation to the next. In Canada, for example, the Organisation of Economic Co-operation and Development identified finding and, more importantly, keeping skilled workers as one of the biggest problems facing companies in the 21st Century. This is a situation that is repeated all over the developed world. And yet, despite widespread recognition that everything is not as it should be, we are not changing the way we do things on any fundamental level at all, but just trying to run harder and faster on the same old treadmill that we have been on since 1856, when Scientific Management was the in thing. The problem is, the more our society changes, the more the nature of work changes, and the more the pendulum swings away from utilising a large number of manual labourers to an increasingly skilled, specialised workforce, the more difficult talent retention is going to become; the more difficult it will be to maintain an organisation's stock of human capital. A factor that is very revealing of the core problem of how we see the people who work for and with us is the language that we have been given to discuss business matters. Even just seeing the problem as "talent retention" or describing skilled individuals as "human capital" is problematic, because describing people merely in terms of their tasks represents one of the biggest shortfalls of Scientific Management; failing to see people as full human beings who need to be fulfilled, respected, and encouraged to grow within the context of their employment.

Why have we resisted change for so long, if just about all of us are very aware that we are not doing things right? Well, change is often good, but it is always frightening, too. It means stepping away from the things we know, questioning our certainties and accepting that many of the things we have always done could be done better or maybe even completely differently. It means accepting that our approach to management may always have been utterly wrong, on any number of levels. It means questioning skills, competencies, and habits of a lifetime that are more than just the way we do things, but a basic element of our very identity, and of the assumptions of the culture we were born into. In other words, it means that we need to question, on a very fundamental level, who we are, what we believe in, and whether our past approach was, just maybe, absolutely rubbish. Of *course* it is bloody hard! It is not supposed to be easy. But, difficult as change can be, the results of change can be wonderfully transformative for organisations, teams, and individuals, and the effort and self-exploration necessary to change are more than worth it.

Another issue that has to be considered is the fact that, the higher up the ranks one goes within any given organisation, the harder it is to change, because the more layers of culturally received knowledge there are to penetrate, explore and, in many cases, discard. Then, the pace at which change is accepted and put into action is variable throughout the company. Ominously, senior management—which inevitably sets the tone for the entire organisation—tends to be the most resistant to change, to actual on-the-ground change as opposed to bells-and-whistles seminars and hand-outs and laminated text about attitudes—even when senior managers are often the ones to recognise that change is necessary, because they are the ones having to answer to their restless shareholders. The problem is that it is not enough to know intellectually when change is necessary. It is also imperative to know it *emotionally* and to be psychologically and practically prepared to do what it takes to make change happen. The latter point is where senior managers typically fall short, for reasons that might not be logical, but that are completely understandable. Having started their own careers in a system in which managers are palpably dominant, powerful figures inspiring awe and yes, maybe a little fear, too, they feel that they have worked long and hard to get to where they are today, and that they want to enjoy it. They *want* that oak desk, that brass plague, and that frisson of power as they sweep past their underlings, Dammnit. Maybe, on a level that they have not quite been able to acknowledge, there is a part of them that kind of likes knowing that the secretaries, accounts clerks, and junior managers are scared when they are called for a meeting. They probably do not realise that all those trappings come with a price, and that is hampered communication between management and employees and, as a result, impeded company performance. Various studies into the psychological effects of what Blanchard has termed "positional" power have concluded that individuals who are in a position of authority over others tend to display traits of preferring unilateral decision-making, an absence of inhibitions, the tendency to act radically and quickly, and the tendency to depersonalise other people. With varying degrees of conscious thought, people in positions of power tend to feel more important; they often even manage to occupy more physical space with their persons by using more expansive body language—stretched out legs, spread arms. I think that these are all characteristics that we have witnessed in the workplace, and possibly also in ourselves. A problem that we all grapple with is the fact that it is easy to forget that power and leadership, while they are often overlapping qualities, are not the same thing. An individual in a position of power over another person has the ability to offer rewards and exact punishment. A leader is someone who has been given a specific social role to bring individuals from point A to point B. In our society, we tend to appoint to leadership positions individuals who display all the trappings of power: dominant body language and speech, self-assurance and certainty, and the tendency to depersonalise others. Anderson and Berdahl describe power as affecting, "a wide range of social behaviours. People with high power have been shown to pay less attention to others and to use stereotypes more, to use less systematic social cognition…to show higher consistency between their internal traits and overt behaviours and to behave in more socially inappropriate ways." What is more, they also identify them as speaking more, initiating physical contact more, and using less complex cognitive processing. One can imagine that these characteristics would not be amiss in a foreman whose job it is to oversee ununionised labourers picking fruit. The problem is that this sort of leadership is no longer as appropriate in today's organisations, with today's highly skilled workers, with some exceptions such as the infantry in the army, which does rely on positional power. The body language, gestures, and speech that all indicate power also indicate a lower level of emotional intelligence, the tendency not to truly listen or empathise and the absence of considerate, aware leadership.

Perhaps senior managers think that they have the most potential to lose when change comes sweeping in, but the truth is that they have the most potential to *win*, because managers who are aware of the drawbacks of using the Scientific Management paradigm in the twenty-first century workplace, and who are ready and prepared to embrace a new way of doing things, will find themselves working within more harmonious, more creative, more stable and, above all, more successful companies.

Yes, senior managers are not aware of all the potential that lies in embracing change. In order for things to become different, senior management has to let go of axioms and habits and beliefs that might as well have been imbibed with their mothers' milk. They have got to accept that they might have to knock their own pedestals down, if they want to experience real respect and communication. They have got to learn how to think differently. They have got to learn how to change the paradigms that they have always operated within. They have got to learn how to rethink their own roles as managers, to find a new way of encapsulating their identity, and a new way of interacting with their employees. Above all, they have got to learn how to enable their employees to access the power implicit in their roles, personalities, and relationships within the organisation, as we shall be discussing later.

To paraphrase the great Bill Clinton, "It is the psychology, stupid."

How management cultures are formed

The reason why it is so very hard for senior management to change is because they have "grown up" as managers within a culture in which much is assumed, and little challenged. They have been working within this culture for so long, they have lost the ability to challenge it, much as the British driver instinctively knows that he should drive on the left side of the road, without having to give the matter much thought. In order to change the way we manage, we have got to start by changing the culture of management.

An experiment in psychology that I have read about involves four monkeys. (Bear with me for a moment; I am not wandering off-topic, I promise!) Now, these monkeys are placed in a cage. In the corner of the cage, up a little staircase accessed through a gate, there are some ripe, delicious bananas.

"Ooh," thinks one of the monkeys. "Bananas! I *love* bananas." And off he goes to retrieve the treat, already happily thinking about how delicious the banana is going to be. But, as he goes through the gate, a trigger is set off, and all the monkeys are sprayed with cold water. Well, they do not like that; not one little bit. Every time one of the monkeys tries to reach the bananas, the same thing happens. Before long, all four monkeys have learned that they should ignore the bananas if they do not want to have a cold shower.

After a while, the researchers take one of the monkeys out and put a new one in. Predictably enough, he tries to reach the bananas. But what happens? Cognizant of the fact that they are about to get sprayed, the other three monkeys do not let him anywhere near the bananas. They jump on him and beat him up. If he tries to do it again, they jump on him again and they beat him even harder. Before long, he has also learned to avoid the bananas. He may not know why the bananas are off-limits, but he certainly knows that he is not fond of being beaten up.

One by one, the researchers replace the monkeys until none of the original monkeys remain. Nobody has actually been sprayed by water, and nobody can even remember having seen another monkey being sprayed. But they still, in the absence of any real threat, do not go anywhere near the bananas, because if there is one thing those monkeys know, it is that you do not go near the bananas in the corner.

What has happened? A culture has been created, and has been handed down from generation to generation.

The problem we have in management today is exactly the same. Each generation of managers is taught how to behave by the generation before— and woe betide the junior manager who tries to restructure everything. He might not be literally beaten up, but that does not mean that senior management is not going to be down on him like a tonne of...well, bananas. Not because his ideas are wrong, and not because they do not like him, but because his suggestions fly in the face of a culture of management that seems to be as immutable as the laws of gravity.

Why does management tend to be so intransigent?

Management finds it hard to change because the culture of management has taught, from one generation to the next, certain "truths" about how things are done that are rarely—if ever—questioned, because they have become so fundamental to our understanding of how things are supposed to be done. One would think that when Moses had finished reading out the Ten Commandments, he had pulled another tablet out of his pocket and continued with the Dogma of Management.

Within the context of the Scientific Management paradigm that currently reigns, we can see two basic subdivisions of managerial style:

Pushing and pulling

In management today, there are basically two styles of doing things. We have what we can call the "push" style and what we can call the "pull" style.*

Let us pause for a moment to consider what these two words mean. A perusal of the dictionary offers the following:

❖ **Push:** to press against with force in order to drive or impel

❖ **Pull:** to exert force upon so as to cause or tend to cause motion toward the force

It is worth noting that when one pushes, the pushed object is moved further away from the pusher, whereas when one pulls, the object and

---

* The terms "push" and "pull" with respect to management styles derive from John Whitmore's book, Coaching for Performance.

the puller come closer together, or move at the same pace and in the same direction.

Managers who pull tend to be more inclusive, while those who push are directive. Managers who pull find themselves constantly at a remove from the people working for them, while those who pull move in the same direction as their employees and find it easier to be close to them in terms of aspirations, goals, and priorities. In the workplace, "Pull" managers will come across as approachable, encouraging and inclined to let individuals and teams work under their own steam, when their results show that they are doing well. "Push" managers will be less concerned with the outward trappings of power and authority. They will be more likely to see themselves as members of the team, rather than as heads of the team. They will say things like: "We have not being doing as well as we could. Let us put our heads together and see if we can think of ways in which we can help each other to be more productive." "Push" leaders are likely to use implicit or explicit threats to manage: "If we do not start making more money around here, heads will roll!" They are more likely to maintain distance—physical and emotional—from the individuals whom they are managing, and more likely to take pride in things like fancy offices and brass plaques. Both styles of management, however, currently take place primarily within the increasingly useless framework of Scientific Management, so even the manager who pulls the most fervently, so to speak, knows that his work is not yielding all the benefits it could.

We can explore how beliefs influence behaviour by getting inside the minds of managers belonging to these two camps. Consider the manager whose behaviour is all about pushing people to where he wants them to go. These are people who can really come across as office dictators, not unlike the old-style bank manager I described before. They are completely in the sway of the psychological effects of power that we have described. Nowadays, the physical and emotional well-being of all employees has to be respected, because we have laws and regulations that protect people from abuse in the workplace, but one gets the impression that the manager who is all about "push" would rather that that was not the case. It often seems that they would be far happier if they literally held the destiny of their workers in the palm of their hand, and it is clear that they respect their own views, opinions, and expertise infinitely more than they respect anyone else's. When the company is in a crisis situation, they threaten employees with terrible fates. When it is going well, they take the credit. When change is necessary, they dictate how and why it will occur. So why are they behaving in this way? It all comes down to the set of beliefs they subscribe to. One thing these managers always come out with is time: "I do not have time. I do not have time to listen. I do not have time to worry about how you are feeling. I have to get the job done. I have to sort people out. I have to hit my numbers. My in-tray..." Another big button is the issue of control and the sense that if the manager is not in control 100%, something is amiss: "I am *expected* to be in control. I am the manager. I would look weak if I did things in any other way, and I need to look strong all the time. I need to have control of what is going on around here."

Let us look at an example of how this management style ends up selling everybody short, including the self-same manager.

A credit card division of Citibank called "Associates" offers credit services to the lower end of the market in the United Kingdom. They have a strong focus on direct, high-pressure sales when dealing with their share of the lending market, which means that their salespeople have to do cold-calling, visiting housing estates and flats, knocking on doors, and offering their credit services to people directly. It can be a stressful job, and it is both physically and emotionally draining, calling for a lot of persistence and well-honed people skills and emotional intelligence. When Associates wanted to look at ways to improve their performance, they called me in, and I ran a coaching programme for them with the manager and his seven direct sales reporters. There was a feeling that things could be going much better than they were. When we had completed a group coaching exercise, I asked the group to think about a specific problem. We went around the group so that each person could discuss what their motivation was to deal with the specific problem. Each of the seven members of staff present had a very low level of motivation to deal with the issue, while the manager's motivation was extremely high. I asked the group what their specific challenges were, and each of the seven staff members said that their problem was increasing sales. That was fairly straightforward, but what was a little puzzling was their low level of motivation to do so. Surely the salespeople should have been the ones most motivated to improve their own performance? The reason why motivation levels were so low soon became clear. The manager was very directive, a bit of a bully in the workplace, and was used to using fear as a mechanism to get people out and selling. Because of his approach, the people working for him had low levels of motivation, because although they all had good ideas, they had an extremely developed fear of failure, and of getting in trouble with their boss if they made an innovative step only for it not to yield immediate, substantial rewards.

When the situation was unveiled to the boss, he was literally appalled by the way his employees saw him, and protested that he did not intend to appear like that at all. This was an individual who understood on paper how important team work was, and who was well able to express in words how and why working together was so important. He had not understood, however, that his words about how everyone had to be a team, working and playing together, did not mean very much unless they were followed up with real, tangible behaviours that demonstrated that he actually *believed* what he was saying. Instead, his behaviour—dogmatic, aggressive and inflexible—spoke legions about the beliefs he really held about his own role in the organisation. Until he addressed these issues, this manager's staff was never going to be able to make a shift towards becoming more motivated. They were never going to become enabled to move beyond their fear of being punished for stepping out of line.

As you can imagine, it is painfully difficult for a manager with such a firm belief in his own ultimate authority and the validity of his culture of management to contemplate change, even when he knows that if the organisation does not do something radical, it is going down the tubes. In the case of the sales manager we have just met, his culture of management had been formed when, as a young salesman, he himself had been metaphorically beaten into submission every day and had survived, while many of his colleagues had left the organisation. It was not surprising that this was the attitude towards management that he was bringing with him.

At its most basic, the problem that holds back so many organisations today lies in a failure to understand that change has to begin with senior management, not with the workers on the shop floor, the salespeople on the street, or the wet-behind-the-ears new managers, fresh from business school. When managers say that they are expected to be in control, because if they do not tell everyone what to do, nothing will get done, they are usually making an accurate assessment of the situation. In most companies where this sort of management prevails, it *is* true that employees will look to their managers for clear, explicit direction as to what they should do, because if they act on their own initiative, they are almost certainly going to get in trouble. They may well have seen a hapless colleague attempting to suggest something he has thought of, and seen him being bawled out for having the temerity to have an independent mind. This sort of environment in turn leads to a situation in which creativity and innovative thought are not encouraged, with the result that the workforce is hampered. But why do employees look to the manager for explicit direction? In fact, this is a classic catch-22 situation. The more the manager insists on absolute power and authority, the less enabled to be creative and smart the employees will feel, and the more directive instruction they will need to get the job done. And so on *ad infinitum*, until or unless something radical happens to shake things up.

So much for "push" management styles. But how are "pull" managers faring in the contemporary workplace? Conversely, the manager who is 100% pull is engaging. This is a manager who believes in teamwork, inclusivity, empowerment, and the axiom that the sum of the parts will create more. This manager is likely to get a better answer when he or she asks a team for input. This manager believes in development and in trust, and his or her workers will work better because when you trust someone, they generally repay that trust. When these managers talk about time, they believe that their approach may take more work at the beginning, but that it will be better and quicker in the long run. They are not hung up about control, because they know that most work is teamwork and they believe in teams. They are not afraid of asking for information when they do not know something, because they do not believe that they have to look all-powerful, all of the time. They create an environment in which creativity and individual spark are rewarded.

So who is pushing and who is pulling?

Neil Rackham, a well-known business writer, posited that the average manager spends 80% of their time engaged in "push" and 20% in "pull" behaviour; certainly statistics that would seem consistent with my experience as a management consultant. What Rackham saw when he looked at successful managers, however—at the 10% at the top—was that they spent much, much more time engaged in "pull" behaviours; 60% pushing and 40% pulling. When he looked at the top 5%, he found that they were using 40% of their time pushing and 60% pulling. Instead of telling people what to do, they were engaging them and asking questions. Now that makes for some very interesting reading!

Even a cursory glance at push and pull management styles makes it pretty obvious which approach is better adapted to the modern workplace, and which is more accommodating and welcoming of change.

The vast majority of managers today subscribe, at least in theory, to the notion that they should be fostering an environment within which effort and creativity are rewarded. The funny thing is that when you talk to most managers, and ask them, "So, what do you believe?" they will answer with a lot of fine words about teams and inclusivity. They talk up "push" behaviour and stress that they care about their employees' emotional well-being, about team-building and all the rest of it.

But what happens when you go into the organisation and look at what is actually going on? What do you see when you observe how the very same manager is interacting with his or her employees? As a management consultant, it is my job to look at organisations and explore what they are doing, and how they are doing it. Typically, I find managers who know that things are not working as well as they should, who recognise that "pull" qualities are infinitely more desirable, but who are finding it almost impossible to effect real change, because they are entangled in the archaic push management culture that is causing so much trouble in the workplace.

People like to *think* that they believe in behaving in an inclusive manner, but very few of them actually *do* believe in this. Managers talk "push" words, but they exhibit "pull" behaviour. Rather than letting people find the answer by themselves, they give directions. They do not really believe in the things they say they believe in, although they might honestly think that they do. Instead, their real beliefs are so dominant that they eliminate all other beliefs when it comes down to actually working, and they set up roadblocks that make lasting change all but impossible. Why? The truth is that it is nobody's fault. I am not saying that we should change our managers; far from it. What we have to do is make possible a culture of management that is more flexible, and more respectful of employees and of changes necessary to the workplace. The difficulties that managers experience with disengaging from an authoritative management style are simply the result of being forced to work within a culture of management that is no longer relevant.

In the army, officers are kept separately from the team, because they know the power of the unit working together. They also know that when and if that team needs to be led in war, the soldiers do not need to be encouraged to think too much, and should be prepared to just do what the officer tells them. The officer is never going to be part of the team, because an officer should be directive.

But business is not the army, and doing business well should not be like going to war. Businesses should be run differently. And that, in a nutshell, is why businesses are going to have to change on some very fundamental levels, starting with the management. Managers set the tone of the whole organisation. They way they behave—whether they exhibit "push" or "pull" behaviours—will be modelled at every level throughout the organisation. When a company decides that it is time to change the way it is run, the first thing that needs to take place is a substantial shift in attitudinal behaviours on the part of the managers.

Of course, we cannot expect people to be able to change effectively within an organisation unless they are provided with the information they need, and communicating this information effectively is clearly key. Communication, however, is something that many of us find difficult—and we might well be even worse at it than we think!

One of the exercises I carry out as a management consultant goes like this: I ask a manager and one of his or her employees to come forward. For the first part of the exercise, the manager is asked to lie on the floor and pretend to be a Martian who has just come to Earth for the first time. As a first-time tourist among human beings, our Martian does not know how to do any of the things we humans take for granted, such as, in this case, standing up from a lying position. He knows the names of the various body parts and can understand simple instructions such as "left" and "right" but that is as far as it goes, leaving any instruction open to very literal interpretation. The employee has to get the "Martian" to stand up, using nothing other than spoken instruction. They are not allowed to physically show them anything. Of course, this is a very complicated activity, and what usually happens is that the poor Martian on the floor ends up adopting a range of positions that might have come from the Karma Sutra, while failing absolutely to stand up. Everyone laughs as they bend over backwards in their literal application of the speaker's instructions. Then, the roles are swapped, and what usually happens this time is that the communication is even worse. The person who is now the Martian follows the literal interpretations to the letter, to the extent that standing up is impossible.

One of the main points of the exercise is that, while the person giving directions might look like the one in charge of the situation, the power actually lies with the person following them, because it is their decision to apply a literal application of their instructions, determining how the exercise is going to pan out. The fact that the people who are partaking in the exercise do worse the second time around is a useful reminder of how we learn; in this case, what the employee has learned from his or her manager is how to be obtuse, confusing, and lacking in clarity!

Creating a healthier culture of management begins with changing belief

In order to help managers change the way they behave, the idea of time has to be tackled, and so do beliefs about the nature and use of control. This is not easy. Just like our monkeys in a cage, the typical manager's experience will be of having been leapt upon and beaten up—in a manner of speaking—every time he has deviated from the long-established norm. Over the years, he has learned not to even try, just like our monkey. He has learned to stick within accepted parameters, even if everyone knows that they are not working out, and even if the organisation has reached crisis point. This behaviour, and the set of beliefs that supports it, has become second nature to the extent that it is almost as difficult to question it as to question fundamental realities in our world, such as gravity or the spherical nature of the planet.

The problems with just about all of the management fads that we have seen come and go is that they focus on behaviour; on doing something differently, or on not doing something. They focus on surface activity rather than the deep, strong currents that create the very nature of the organisation. They tend not to look at the origins of those behaviours, those surface activities. They tend not to look at why we behave in a certain way, and not another. They do nothing to challenge the fundamentals of our culture of management. They tell us that we have to run faster without exploring why, no matter how fast we run, we seem to stay on the same spot.

When an individual attends therapy for a particular behavioural problem—let us say, for a tendency towards domestic violence—the therapist has a two-fold task. First of all, he has to get Individual X to stop beating up his spouse. That is clearly an imperative, even if it means calling in the police and restricting individual X's freedom. Secondly, and in the longer term even more importantly, the therapist has to help Individual X understand *why* he reacts to stress by beating up his spouse, because only when he understands the reasons and beliefs behind his behaviours will he be enabled to stop engaging in them. It may be that Individual X witnessed similar behaviour growing up, that he has problems with authority, or that he is desperately afraid of his wife leaving him. Whatever the case, once he understands how an erroneous belief system has contributed to his behaviour, he can work on learning how to develop a different, healthier way of reacting to stress in his environment. In other words, for long-lasting change, it is not enough to punish him for his behaviour, or propose a new set of behaviours, it is necessary to help Individual X to change his personal culture.

In a very similar way—and without suggesting that they are prone to physical violence!—managers can only change their managerial style in the longer term by exploring how and why their belief system around management evolved, by looking at the management culture in which they have always worked, and of which they are now a part, and by envisioning what a more useful management culture would look like. Once they understand the origins and context of their behaviour, they can choose to move beyond it.

So, when we look at reforming management in our businesses today, we have got to forget about trying to change behaviours and look at how we can change beliefs instead. When the beliefs change, the behaviour will follow.

The team meeting

Let me give you an example. All companies run team meetings. Usually, these are headed up by the manager who sets the time, place, agenda and tone of the meeting. Woe betide the employee who does not respect the all-important meeting. These meetings are often anticipated with anxiety, and even dread. In their aftermath, employees often huddle crossly around the office coffee machine, mulling over what the boss said, and muttering about how they think he should be handling things differently, and how they would do things, if only they were in his position. Of course, they will not share these views of how things could be done with their manager—not in a million years!—because they do not want to be yelled at, ridiculed, or otherwise made to look less than competent in front of their co-workers. I am sure that you have been there and done that, because who has not?

It rarely occurs to anybody that things could or should be handled any differently.

This is where people like me come in. It is our job to look at things from the outside and pose tricky questions; questions that probably have not been asked before, because they chip away at the foundations of everything managers think they know and take for granted. Let us stick with our example, the shibboleth that is the manager-run team meeting.

When I turn to managers and ask, "So, why do *you* run the team meeting? Why not somebody else?" I am generally answered with a baffled stare, and the stammered words, "Well…but…I am the manager…I mean…it is expected of me. Isn't it?" It is as if I had asked the manager why he gets dressed in the morning, rather than coming into work in his pyjamas.

"But you want to be part of the team?" I ask. "Or did I misunderstand something?"

"Of course! I am a firm believer in the importance of team work." (At this stage, the manager will typically rattle off a few of the key "pull" attributes he would like to think he believes in.)

"Yes," I will say, "but as soon as you sit at the head of the table, behaving like 'the manager' you are not *going* to be part of the team. And nobody is going to feel completely free to discuss anything with you, because you are the boss, you are in charge and you are making everybody feel nervous!" (At this point, my observation may be met with a few embarrassed chuckles from the staff, who recognise themselves in this analysis.)

So why *does* the manager have to run the team meeting? Why? The only real reason is: "Because that is the way it has always been done." In other words, the only thing preventing us from holding team meetings differently is a belief that derives from nothing more substantial than historical precedent—in other words, an aspect of management culture—and all we have to do to start holding team meetings differently is change the underlying belief that says that it is not a team meeting unless the manager is sitting at the top of the table, setting the agenda.

Instead, if we want staff members to feel more responsible and inclusive, what managers should do is attend meetings on the same level as everyone else, and give the chairmanship of it to a member of the team. "You create the agenda!" they will say. "You, John from accounts or Brenda from sales, are the team leader for the next hour."

So what happens then? Is the king dethroned? Do all the members of staff suddenly realise that the emperor is naked? Does the intrepid manager lose his aura of authority?

Will things never be the same again?

Well, the manager may find that the team will put things on the agenda that he or she does not consider to be important, and this may be quite startling for him or her. But the fact is that these things *are* important, because they matter to the team, and if they are not dealt with, they will continue to impact on the way the team works. By sitting at the head of that table every time there is a team meeting, the manager is failing to identify and deal with all of the things that are of real concern. Instead, by enabling somebody else to take the lead for a change, issues that are worrying the employees, and that previously might only have been aired in the coffee room or down the pub after work, are taken out and looked at and shaken out and, often, dealt with. What happens is that the manager is giving a message that is crystal clear, that tells employees that what they feel and think matters, and that their opinions and views are of enormous importance. Purely by putting someone else in charge of the meeting, the whole dynamic within the team has been changed. It sounds simple enough, but in order for a manager to become enabled to cede the driving seat once in a while, they have got to eliminate their expectations of "being the boss" and all that they think that will entail. The new way of doing things will create a whole different set of emotions, and represents a paradigm shift in behaviour.

Emotional intelligence and contemplating change

Without change, there is atrophy, so change is an essential feature of living and working. Whatever one does, and whatever the size of one's organisation, change is a constant. But the fact that change is both necessary and ubiquitous does not mean that it is accepted at every, or even *any*, level within an organisation. Quite the reverse. When one goes into any organisation, and talks with the people within it, discussion invariably come around to the topic of what has changed, what is about to change, and why everybody is anxious and upset at the prospect of change. Change is always a burning topic, and a drain on company resources and time, and many changes are instigated practically against the will of almost everyone within the organisation. But by seeing change as an inevitable and usually positive aspect of company and individual development, it can become an opportunity, or series of opportunities, rather than an obstacle.

Effecting change within organisations is such a difficult issue that an entire branch of psychology is devoted to the issue of change management. When changes—personal or organisational—are announced, attitudes are formed on the basis of a combination of instinctive, emotional responses, and rational thought. Change can be seen as progress, opportunity and innovation, but it can also be interpreted as causing fear and anxiety and as being demoralising.

Key to succeeding in effecting change is the level of emotional intelligence within the organisation. Now, the term "emotional intelligence", might sound rather fluffy and vague, but research has shown that the level of emotional intelligence present in an organisation is an excellent predictor of success. In a 1999 study, Boyatzis looked at a number of experienced partners in a multinational consulting firm, exploring their performance in light of their emotional intelligence, as well as other competencies. The partners who scored high for emotional intelligence delivered $1.2 million more profit from their accounts than did other partners—a 139 percent incremental gain. There is nothing fluffy and vague about that! Also in 1999, McClelland looked at the performance of division presidents in a drinks company. Prior to the company's decision to start selecting division presidents on the basis of qualities rooted in emotional intelligence, 50% of these had left or been made to leave, because they were not performing well. After emotional intelligence became a deciding factor, this dropped to just 6%. Again, these are tangible, meaningful results that point to the immense importance of "soft" factors like emotional intelligence.

The fact is that all other things—such as I.Q., training, number of years on the job and skill level—workers and managers with higher levels of emotional intelligence will *always* perform better, because they are better able to interpret subtleties of behaviour, better at communicating, better at understanding the motives behind their own behaviour, and better at negotiating the maze of human relationships that makes up an organisation. A simple way of understanding emotional intelligence is to see it as comprised of self-awareness and social awareness, which lead in turn to better self-management and relationship management alike. In the context of a modern organisation composed mostly of knowledge workers who need to be engaged and rewarded both emotionally and practically, these are skills that are invaluable.

One of my previous clients is BBC Technology, which is the organisation responsible for creating bbc.co.uk, a highly respected website in the world of news and media. I was involved at the point at which the technical side of the organisation was being merged with the commercial side, in order to form a more homogenous group of two very different types of people. It was my responsibility to work with the computer staff who were responsible for the technical side of things, to help them with any issues relating to the change that threatened to destabilise their relationship with management and their performance in the workplace.

When I arrived at the technical headquarters of BBC Technology, the people whom I met were all remarkably intelligent, bright individuals, who knew their computers and the technical side of things inside out. Most of them were very young, and they lived and breathed computers. When they were not working, they were spending their coffee breaks programming, or leafing avidly through *Wired* magazine. Probably because they were spending so much time interacting with machines, most of the technical staff of BBC Technology had very limited skills when it came to interacting with other human beings. The role they played in their organisation was crucial, but their difficulties in expressing themselves and handling their own emotions were set to cause problems in the new situation in which they were about to find themselves. I am not stating it too strongly when I say that their ability to change was almost non-existent. On the commercial side, the sales and other employees were almost the exact opposite of their technically-minded colleagues. They were dressed to impress, with keen personal skills that they brought to their work, which mostly involved interacting directly with other human beings. The two sets of people had serious difficulty getting on in the office. They were all speaking English, but they might as well have been speaking different languages. When the promised change started to happen, the technical staff found it enormously difficult, because they had never been able to discuss the problems they were experiencing, beyond presenting management with sulky expressions and indecipherable grunts. There were practical issues at hand—they were moving to another town and would have to find new places to live and new pubs to drink in—but most difficult for them was the fact that they did not have the emotional intelligence skills to think about *what* they were doing, *why* they were doing it and *what they needed* in order to make it easier. They were pissed off, they disappeared into corners in a huff, and they generally displayed behaviour appropriate to a kindergarten. Dealing with this inarticulate mutiny was a serious challenge for the management of BBC Technology.

While much has been written on the emotions that accompany change, less attention is typically given to the emotions involved in managing change and, more specifically, to creating the emotional conditions that enable managers to be very sensitive to the way that change is affecting the people managed. An integral part of managing change is seeing through not just the new ways of doing things, but also managing the emotions that are produced in the process. While this is something that good managers already do to varying degrees, more or less unconsciously, acquiring a more in-depth awareness of the issue is valuable.

Any organisation that is considering major change will spend a lot of time thinking about the macro-management of the issue. They will paint a picture of the future using broad strokes, and communicate it to the staff using sweeping statements. They may say things like, "I know it will be difficult for a little while but we will all be better off soon." The practical problems suffered by staff will be brushed aside as incidental and, in any case, not really the business of the organisation. But the majority of employees will experience change at the micro-level; it will translate to many small differences in the way they approach their work every day and even the way they live outside work—picking the kids up from school, getting home later and having to organise more child-care, finding it difficult to arrange holidays during important times of the year or whatever—and each difference will have to be integrated with all the others, until they have arrived at a productive, useful approach. Managing this myriad of small changes is vital, because not implementing change at a micro-level will have profound repercussions throughout the organisation. Doing so with emotional intelligence makes it infinitely easier to promote useful strategies. The emotionally intelligent individual is not the one who rigorously promotes a one-sided view of change. Instead, the ability to view an issue from all angles, including understanding the reasons behind some people's pessimism and lack of enthusiasm, makes it easier to frame the challenges of change in an encouraging light. Emotional intelligence also recognises that people can feel more than one sentiment at the same time. For example, the employee can simultaneously express the feelings: "I want to make these changes because they are good for the company and the company has always been good for me," and "I don't want to make these changes, because I am afraid that they will reduce my autonomy and free time," and even, "I would like to make these changes, but nobody else does, and I don't want to stand out…"

While employee ambivalence towards or fear of change can be very destructive, ignoring it or treating it with hostility is not the answer.

When you, as a manager, make a decision to change your company's style of management from old-fashioned Scientific Management to something more adapted to the modern world, emotional intelligence—both yours and that of those you work with—will be your most valuable asset.

Tapping in to emotional intelligence

In order to embrace change, company managers and employees need to understand what emotional intelligence is, and learn how to foster it within their organisation. It is not a secret that one of the main attributes that distinguishes successful from less successful organisations is the level of emotional intelligence within the group. So exactly what is emotional intelligence? According to Goleman, it is composed of five core emotional competencies:

❖ The ability to identify and name one's emotional states and to understand what connects emotions, thought and action.

❖ The ability to manage emotional states, not to "fly off the handle" and to be able to identify less than useful emotional states and transform them.

❖ The ability to enter into emotional states associated with a drive to achieve and be successful—the resourceful emotions that we discussed above.

❖ The capacity to interpret, recognise and influence the emotional states of other people.

❖ The ability to start and continue healthy relationships with other people.

Emotional intelligence is a quality that we all have, although it may be more pronounced in some people than in others. We can compare it to the ability to walk. All able-bodied adults can walk, but they are not all going to become professional athletes or hardcore mountaineers. At the one end of the emotional intelligence scale, we find people with severe autism, a condition characterised by the inability to empathise with others, and at the other people with such a degree of empathy that they are likely to burst into tears when they hear about the troubles that somebody else has been facing. The majority of us have a range of skills around emotional intelligence, filtered through factors such as gender, culture, and circumstance, but exclusive to no particular demographic. Individuals may differ in the extent to which they display emotional intelligence, but this quality can be fostered and encouraged, just as we can all become fitter and stronger, even if we are not going to be Olympic material. It can be "tapped into" and a business environment can be created in which the members of that organisation feel able to use their emotional intelligence in their interactions with the people around them, and in forming decisions. What is more, empirical research has shown that investing in coaching to enhance emotional intelligence skills translates into real, tangible, measurable benefits to the organisation.

One of the many clients with whom I have worked over the years is the LifeScan element of the Johnson and Johnson group. LifeScan is an organisation dedicated to the production and use of products and devices intended to improve the quality and length of life of individuals with diabetes. LifeScan introduced me to the specialised nurses who were the ones to interact directly with clients with diabetes

Diabetes is a condition that often presents early in life—during childhood, adolescence and early adulthood. At this stage, it often does not seem to affect the individual that much at all. However, the way the diabetic person treats their body now has profound repercussions for their future health and standard of living, and this is a message that is crucial to communicate.

When I started talking to the nurses, I realised that the most important thing they could bring to the company/client interface was not their medical know-how or their familiarity with LifeScan's products, but their emotional intelligence. In their meetings with clients, they typically had only a very short time to spend with each person, and during that time their role was to educate them on the subject of how to monitor their diabetes, how to mitigate against its effects, and why it was so important to do so. Many of the nurses found their work extremely frustrating. They knew their subject intimately, but they felt that they were not managing to get the message across and that, all too often, they were not making any difference. Faced with a yet another surly eighteen-year-old diabetes patient, they would say, "You have got to keep your alcohol and carbohydrate consumption to a minimum," and would be met with remarks like, "But I feel fine. I love clubbing. What is wrong with going out for a bag of chips?" No matter how hard they tried, the message that drinking too much and eating chips now could mean future amputations, blindness, and sexual dysfunction often seemed to be lost on adolescents and young adults who could not imagine being thirty, let alone fifty-five or seventy. Over the course of a day's work, frustrations would build up until each client/nurse session began with the nurse in a bad place, a place in which his or her emotional intelligence was not being used. You can imagine how effective sessions were when both nurses and clients started their conversation with the underlying thought, "What is the point? This is not going to make any difference, anyway. This person is not interested in me and my knowledge. "

My job was to help the nurses take the reins and become more attuned to self-managing the application of their emotional intelligence, especially when it came to recognising the impact that their mood would have on each patient as they walked into the room. The patient who is already in denial about the potential severity of their condition or upset about an underlying problem that cannot help but influence the way they need to live is much less likely to feel able to openly discuss their health and health management with someone whose stress and irritation are visible and apparent. Another key was becoming more open to understanding, and making accurate interpretations of, client behaviour and mood, to understanding the emotional baggage that clients were bringing to their interaction with the nurse. It was important to realise that the words spoken did not tell the whole story; to be alive to the nuances in the client's words and body language. Underlying emotions of fear and anxiety are often vocalised as aggression and reluctance to change. When the nurses started being able to use their own reactions and behaviour as a model for how they wanted the clients to respond to them, communicating with them became a lot easier. As they learned how to respond to comments such as, "I don't care what happens to me when I am fifty, I just want to have fun now!" by saying, "I know it can be frightening to think about the future when you have diabetes, but it will seem a lot less frightening when you know more about it. What do you think you might like to be doing when you are fifty?" they found that the message was better received and absorbed.

My key role with the nurses was to help them to understand the power of questions and of really listening to the answers provided. Individuals can only change their beliefs if they have a different picture, a different view. The nurses' job in changing beliefs was to alter this mental picture. This was achieved in large part by asking questions.

Fostering emotional intelligence makes change work

Currently, companies differ in the extent to which the individuals within the company are allowed to utilise their personal emotional intelligence. The emotional environment within the company determines how emotionally intelligent the organisation is as a multi-faceted entity. Before contemplating change and formulating a way to deal with it, it is crucial for companies to analyse the extent to which they are emotionally intelligent, and then to create a situation in which awareness is raised at both individual and company level. When an organisation's managers and employees are allowed to express their emotional intelligence, they can react to change by communicating, rather than becoming withdrawn, by looking for the benefits in the change in question, rather than dreading what they fear to be drawbacks and by feeling that within their changing environment they are in a position to make positive choices, rather than being cast adrift on a sea of change that happens to them, whether they want it to or not.

Accessing one's emotional intelligence creates a spectrum of positive emotions and an associated rise in self-esteem. Feeling good makes it easier for the individual within the company to access the best of their skills when necessary, and they are much more able to cope effectively with change.

So how can emotional intelligence be fostered in you, in your team-members, in your organisation? Is emotional intelligence a fixed quality, as some think I.Q. is, or can it be made to grow? While some people may be naturally blessed with higher levels of emotional intelligence, the good news is that everyone—and, by extension, every organisation—can learn how to maximise access to this resource. This starts by fostering an organisation within which both emotional and cognitive learning can occur.

Cognitive learning is, of course, the acquisition of new skills—learning a new computer software, getting to grips with the colour photocopier, or whatever—while emotional learning is about fine-tuning one's ability to access, understand, and influence the emotional states of oneself and others. Personal levels of emotional intelligence derive from a mix of influences: probably in part from our genetic heritage, but largely from habits formed over the course of a lifetime of experiences, and from the intellectual environment that we experience every day. Nowadays, with such a heavy reliance on technologies that make it easier for us to communicate with people without actually having to meet them, we are all at risk for losing the people skills—unconsciously interpreting facial and body language, tone of voice, and so forth—that enable real emotional understanding. The answer to this dilemma does not, of course, lie in ditching all the wonderful technology that has improved our lives in so very many ways, but in remembering to keep our emotional "muscles" toned. We also have to avoid the risk of attributing moral values to our findings. If, for example, you look at your team-member, Waqas, and determine that he is not very good at understanding when people feel awkward because of his tendency to misinterpret their cues, that does not mean that Waqas is a bad or unintelligent person. It may be that he is not the most emotionally intelligent fellow on your team, but then he does not get out of the IT centre very often, and his social skills are pretty rusty. Perhaps the answer lies in getting the whole team together more often, even if only for a cup of coffee several times a week, as well as your periodic team meetings, or to insist that, from now on, team suggestions about change should always be communicated face-to-face as well as, or instead of, by email or office memo. Perhaps the answer can also be found in understanding that the words that are actually spoken do not necessarily represent the complete message, and that hopes and anxieties are not always expressed explicitly at all. Perhaps asking yourself how much you are bringing your own emotional intelligence to bear on your interactions with Waqas will reveal that he is not the only one who could be a little more self-aware.

Above all, one cannot force people to work on their emotional intelligence skills, so managers need to start by working on their own, and dealing with the personal feelings of defensiveness that inevitably result from an honest look at where one is falling short. They may also need to think carefully about their own cultural background, and the extent to which it is impacting on how they communicate with people. Across cultures, people are more similar than they are different, and there are no statistical differences in emotional intelligence between one culture and another, but our ethnicity tends to overlay our emotional expressions and revelations with a veneer of culturally-informed notions about what degree of openness is appropriate. In organisations with branches in different countries, or simply with workers from different ethnic backgrounds, it will be worth looking at the different ways the various cultures represented within the organisation tend to express themselves. Holding a team discussion on this topic may be revealing, and could be a lot of fun.

Regardless of the age or the experiential background of the individual, they can become more emotionally competent if they are given the time and the appropriate environment in which to foster their emotional skills, and if their leader models that he, too, is working on his emotional intelligence.

Of course, deciding that it is time to change an organisation's way of doing things, deciding that it is time to begin creating a new culture of management and work, is just the beginning. Change is a dynamic, living process that must be given the time it needs to happen.

Chapter 4)

What the knowledge worker needs

In the knowledge society the most probable assumption and certainly the assumption on which all organizations have to conduct their affairs is that they need the knowledge worker far more than the knowledge worker needs them—Peter Drucker

What knowledge workers need from their jobs—from their careers—and from their management is very different to the needs of the vanishing breed of unspecialised workers. Scientific Management has long being selling everyone short—workers, management, and society. It is past time we tore up the rule book and invented a new one, one that respects the rights and needs of workers *and* maximises companies' ability to fulfil all of their potential, something that in many quarters is still considered to be impossible, as the old idea of workers and management in constant conflict still holds sway. The outcome of embracing change will reap untold benefits, not just in terms of improved company revenue and a better quality of life for workers and managers alike, but in areas that are rarely considered as part of the manager's remit. By extension, it will help to create a society in which people are expected to be *people*, not robots generating products, services, and products. They—we—will feel happier, more successful and more cherished, and that is good news for us all.

Most of all, in writing this new rule book, we need to understand that the things the typical knowledge worker requires from his or her work environment are not just the bread-and-butter things that management assumes, things as straightforward as a regular salary, a pension plan, and an acceptable physical environment in which to work. As we already pointed out, today a majority of workers in the developed world are knowledge workers, and what they need from their managers is very different from what, in the main, they are receiving.

But why? What is so special about knowledge workers that calls for this sea shift in how we do things? Once again, let us turn to our past to understand where we are at right now.

Investing in skills/opportunity cost

In the first chapter, we mentioned one of the most important cultural changes that occurs when a society becomes agricultural and settles down in one place for the first time. That society begins to invest in an area not just in practical terms—building houses, fertilising the land, and so forth—but also, and even more importantly, *emotionally*. They start to care about their area. They want to make it better and they are not afraid to put in the work necessary to do so. They want to be able to pass on all they have put into their area to their children and grandchildren. They have committed to their area in the long run, and they know that if they keep working at it, it will continue to provide them with their livelihood indefinitely. What is more, they are willing and prepared to put in extra work to ensure that, not only will it continue to provide them with a livelihood, but that that livelihood will grow incrementally bigger with all the extra work they are doing. The early farmers cared so much about their areas that whole belief systems grew up, devoted to protecting and nurturing the land that meant so much for them. Even today, we celebrate Easter and Hallow'een, which are none other than what remains of early festivals created around the crucial agricultural events of sowing and reaping; in other words, around profits and job satisfaction. As the French say: *plus ça change, plus c'est la même cose.*

Just like the first horticulturalists, the knowledge worker has invested emotionally in his or her livelihood, too, whether they are working in medicine or the arts, construction or cooking. They have spent months or, more likely, years acquiring the highly specialised skills that make them what they are today. They have probably invested a lot of money in their education, training, or apprenticeship, either directly or through monies not earned while they were acquiring the skills they would bring to the workplace. When we talk about personal investment in skills, we are not dealing in euphemism. Typically, a knowledge worker will have attended a university, another type of third level educational establishment, or will have worked as an apprentice for a period of some years; maybe all three. During these years, they will have earned little or nothing, as they prepared themselves for a life of skilled labour. Economists recognise this period of no or low earnings as a cost, referred to in economic analyses as "opportunity cost", which means the cost of something in terms of an opportunity forgone. When we are talking about investment in education or training, the greatest cost (at least in Europe, where education is heavily subsidised) is not the fees incurred, but the money not earned during those years. In the shorter term, one could make more money working behind a bar or picking tomatoes; this means that the opportunity cost of a year in education is not just the direct fees incurred but the equivalent of a year's work at minimum wage plus tips! Considering that many knowledge workers spend several years preparing themselves to enter employment, the initial opportunity cost of training is considerable indeed. In the longer term, investing in skills makes sense, and we all know it—but the very real costs and effort involved in acquiring skills make those skills all the more cherished.

Doing what they do today may be the result of a cherished dream that knowledge workers held close to their hearts for years before entering the university or work environment where they would acquire the skills they needed during this learning period. They know that, because of the extra work they put into acquiring their skills, they are better able to provide for themselves and for their families, and they hope that their continuing efforts will reap ever-greater dividends throughout the rest of their working lives. Their identity and self-esteem are inextricably linked to what they do: "I am a solicitor;" "I am a nurse;" "I am a stockbroker;" "I am an agricultural advisor." The sum of their skills is who they are, much more than the colour of their skin or hair, their national identity or their social background, because their skill-set represents something that they have chosen for themselves, and worked hard to obtain. Their skills are like a garden that they have planted and cherished for all of their adult lives, and they have a strong need to see that garden continue to flourish and grow; why else did they put so much effort into planting it? Why else did they forego years of potential earnings to acquire their skills?

When they are managed with care, encouraged to optimise on what they know, and given the opportunity to take both responsibility and recognition for their work, knowledge workers will respond well. But when the opposite occurs—as, alas, it often does—they will take their skills elsewhere or, untended, their skills will no longer be updated, and the worker will start failing to fulfil his or her potential.

Helping knowledge workers to manage themselves

Applying the term "manager" to coordinating the supervisor of knowledge workers is, or should be, a bit of a misnomer, because one of the salient characteristics of these highly trained people is their capacity to self-regulate their work, given the right support and the right environment. The right environment for knowledge workers is one in which they feel secure and safe enough to pose the following questions of themselves: "What are my strengths? What are my weaknesses? Where do I need help? How can I grow?" Under Scientific Management, too many knowledge workers are allowed to labour on with the delusion that their weaknesses do not really matter, because management is there to take care of things, or because, "that is something for another department to worry about," or because they are secretly afraid that showing that they are not all-powerful in their field will make them vulnerable. Instead, when the right atmosphere of openness is created, individuals' capacity to analyse both themselves and their tasks at work is impressive. In a 2000 study, Drucker cites the example of how hospitals can improve the productivity of nurses by giving them more power to self-manage, not less: "...Yet we know that hospitals can improve productivity by asking their nurses two simple questions: What are you being paid for, and how much time do you spend doing that? Typically, nurses say they are paid to provide patient care, or to keep the doctors happy. Both are good answers; the problem is that they have no time to do either job. One hospital more than doubled its nurses' productivity simply by asking them these two questions, and then hiring clerks to do the paperwork that prevented nurses from doing their real job."

One of the most common mistakes made in managing knowledge workers occurs when the organisation's focus remains on productivity. When managers obsess about productivity, they inevitably concentrate their efforts on trying to make people work harder, instead of trying to help them to work better, often resulting in a workforce that is just exhausted from working overtime, and still not producing as well as it could or should. In this sort of environment, resentment towards management tends to be high, and skilled workers are restless, and very inclined to leave when the opportunity presents itself. Effective knowledge workers are given considerable scope to self-manage. In the example above, when nurses were given the opportunity to discuss what they felt should be their priorities for work, they made an accurate assessment of the situation and, with the support of management, were able to radically improve the state of affairs in their workplace.

The complete worker

What happens when the knowledge worker is not nurtured, is not helped to tend their skills, and to develop and grow? The stark reality is that all that intelligence and training and creativity that are so central to their role will start to atrophy. They will get up in the morning and look at themselves in the mirror and say, "This is me. This is as good as it is going to get. From now on, it is just a question of plodding along, until I cannot even plod anymore."

Pretty depressing, eh?

Now, it is bad enough to feel that way when you are seventy, but in an unfulfilling work environment these feelings are deeply unproductive to the person affected and, by extension, to everything they do and everyone they work with, regardless of how talented and skilled they are. The same feelings will bleed into their lives outside work, too, affecting the way they interact with the people they care about, and their very quality of life, today and in the future. Too many people are feeling that way in their forties, thirties, and even twenties. "This is as good as it is going to get," is a feeling that leads inexorably towards vegetation, chronic dissatisfaction, and the conviction that one is unsuccessful, *by definition.* Just as the fulfilled knowledge worker derives satisfaction and self-identity from the fact that they work in a given role, and do so well, the knowledge worker who feels unsuccessful will inevitably work simply to make ends meet—to pay that mortgage, cover those utility bills and pay for the groceries. They will cease tending their garden of skills, and will view the company they work for as a treadmill on which they have to spend a certain amount of time every day—or else.

It sounds depressing, does it not? But far too many people are working in order to make ends meet when what we need is for people to *work* in order to *live*. We spend a third of our lives at work, and half of our waking lives. Work should be a place where the knowledge worker grows and finds emotional and psychological fulfilment, as well as recognition and the possibility to develop new skills, and progress towards where he or she wants to be.

When the goals are right, the effort will grow to match them

When one's environment is rewarding, stimulating and fulfilling, acquiring new skills, performing better, and learning more all become surmountable challenges. When a goal is desired, doing the work necessary to reach it does not become magically easier, but it ceases to be an unwelcome burden.

Let me give you an example. When I was a little boy, I longed to be a pilot. I could not imagine anything more exciting than getting behind the controls of a plane, and soaring up into the sky. Unfortunately, when I was thirteen, I discovered that I was colour blind. And that was that: no professional pilot's licence for me!

Later, as an adult, I decided that I would learn how to fly. To my dismay, I realised that I would have to master a lot of technical expertise, which is not something that comes easily to me at all. I had to understand the mechanics of how a plane flies, understand the engine, and know about the aerodynamics of stresses and forces—and I had to pass an exam in order to get permission to fly on my own. All of that meant that I had to spend hours studying. Usually, poring over topics that I do not find particularly easy is not exactly my favourite activity, but because I was connected to the vision of myself flying, and understood what all the studying and sitting the exam meant for me, I was able to study and do whatever it took to pass the test. My focus was on the end result, and I was completely connected to my vision.

In the workplace, too, we need to understand that knowledge workers must be connected to a vision; not just the vision of the company which must be, in one way or another, to make more money, but also to a personal vision of themselves within the company, growing, developing their skills, and finding the recognition and support that all human beings require. We need to learn how to treat people more holistically and understand that the way their lives unfold outside work has profound repercussions for what they need from work, and vice versa.

Let us explore an example, rather simplistically based on the sort of interaction that might happen in the workplace. Imagine the worker who goes to her manager with a request: "I want to ask for some leave. I would like to go on holiday."

Our manager (we will call her "Kate") does not even look up from her desk: "No, Barbara. I'm sorry. We are short-staffed. It is just going to have to wait. Is that all?"

Barbara stands there for a moment, and then she mutters, "Yeah, sure," and shuffles away.

From this interaction, which has not lasted for more than a minute, it is very clear that the manager does not really care about Barbara, beyond seeing her as someone who is just going to have to put her head down and plug away at her tasks. The company is short-staffed, so the answer to Barbara's request for a holiday is "no". In short, she has been dealt with in a very shoddy, inefficient way by the management of her organisation. Kate does not care how Barbara is feeling, or how badly she might really need that holiday. Maybe Barbara is exhausted. Maybe she has not taken a break for six months. Maybe she has just gone through an acrimonious divorce, or lost a parent. Perhaps her child is having problems, and needs to be with a parent for a week or two. Maybe Barbara just needs a couple of weeks in the sun to recharge her batteries. Whatever the reason, the bottom line is that the company does not care. The company is only interested in the short term. The company wants Barbara's bum on her office chair, and that is that.

What is wrong with this scenario? The short answer? Everything, and not just from Barbara's point of view. If our manager is going to get the best out of Barbara, she needs to be paid more than lip service.

If we are going to get the best from our staff, we need to start seeing them in the wider context of their lives, their aspirations, and their emotional as well as physical needs. In the context of a world in which the customer's needs, and the customer's experience of a company have become paramount, we need to see our employees as our customers, as consumers of the management, coaching, and leadership that we can offer, in a context in which everybody understands, and takes as read, that effort and dedication will be acknowledged and rewarded. Why does the knowledge worker come to work at a given organisation? One reason is, of course, because they need money to live, and want to draw the salary that the organisation has to offer. Another reason is because they believe that the organisation offers them the opportunity to grow, mature, and develop as working individuals. They may be attracted by training or promotion opportunities, or look on the organisation as a good place to hone skills before moving elsewhere. In this respect, the knowledge worker is effectively a customer of the organisation, who pays with their work—with their actual output and with their creative and technical knowledge—for certain services, only one of which is the salary.

In management, the dictum that should be followed is not, of course, "the customer is always right." It is that it is the manager's job to serve the customer. It is the manager's job to ensure that employees find that their positions offer them the rewards and potential they have a right to expect, above and beyond the financial reward that is their salary. All customers judge the businesses they interact with. When we go out for a meal with our friends, we leave talking about the quality of the food and the level of service. If a shop assistant is rude to us, we are likely not to visit that shop again. Employees also judge their organisation's real approach to its workers not just by what managers say, but by what they do; by whether managers have a service approach to their employees or not. Just like any customers, employees exercise customer choice: "Will I stay and let the company take advantage of my skills for a lengthy period, or will I put in the time here while circling job advertisements in the newspaper during my lunch break?" The message they receive from their managers will help them to decide.

In order to promote a "customer service" attitude towards employees, managers need to use their own behaviour to create a model for behaviour in the workplace, and remember to treat employees with the same courtesy and care extended to customers. As customers, employees should never be belittled, they should instead be encouraged to bring problems and ideas for solutions to the attention of their managers, helped to find time for discussing issues at hand with management and with each other and, above all, experienced and known as idiosyncratic, individual men and women.

So what happens when companies stick to Scientific Management at the expense of changing the organisation's culture of management? In fact, not adopting a customer-service approach costs a lot of money in terms of lost contracts and rapid employee turnover. Failing to understand and respect the need of knowledge workers—failing to develop an effective customer-service based network of relationships within the workplace—is a problem that is affecting business all over the world in very real, tangible terms. In 2006, no less an authority than the Economist reported that:

> "…a large and growing number of businesses…from consulting to hedge funds…run on brainpower. When the Corporate Executive Board (CEB), a provider of business research and executive education based in Washington, DC, recently conducted an international poll of senior human-resources managers, three-quarters of them said that "attracting and retaining" talent was their number one priority. Some 62% worried about company-wide talent shortages. The CEB also surveyed some 4,000 hiring managers in more than 30 companies, and was told that the average quality of candidates had declined by 10% since 2004 and the average time to fill a vacancy had increased from 37 days to 51 days. More than one-third of the managers said that they had hired below-average candidates "just to fill a position quickly". The CEB found, too, that about one in three employees had recently been approached by another firm hoping to lure them away."

Managers know that the Economist's report is true, and most are painfully aware of how difficult it is to hold on to talented workers. And yet, far too many are reacting to their employees in the manner I have just described. This, unfortunately, is a situation that I am familiar with from my own professional background.

Within a company I used to work for, the style of management was very much a dictat. Management was secretive, rather than inclusive. Things happened behind closed doors and were kept from employees. Management did not ask their community what they were working for and, as a consequence, they created such profound levels of dissatisfaction that people left long before they had fully explored their potential within the organisation. At that time, I was in charge of providing a service to a specific country in the organisation's remit. I had a problem of long standing with one of the individuals working there. When I decided that I needed them to do something, they did not want to do it and went in turn to senior management. Without taking any time to explore the reasoning behind the decision that I had taken, senior management arrived at what they saw as a compromise. I was not involved in the decision-making process, undermining my position with the member of staff, and leaving me feeling frustrated because my needs were not being respected by senior management. In the event, the employee was unhappy, I was unhappy, and eventually both of us left, which of course made senior management unhappy because now we had to be replaced. The problem boiled down to the fact that our senior manager was looking at short-term solutions to long-term challenges, rather than engaging with the people working for him, and working with them to find solutions to the challenges in the workplace. In another case, a colleague who was based on Scotland had to travel a huge amount, spending days and even weeks away from his home and family. He was an excellent employee, but the more he had to travel the more his quality of life suffered, until he was, quite literally, feeling desperate. Time and time again, he went to senior management, and tried to discuss ways in which he could continue working without having to travel as much. Time and time again, he was told that they could worry about that later, and that for now the important thing was to keep bringing the money in. Before long, this hugely talented individual left and went into business on his own, sacrificing a certain amount of earnings for a vastly improved lifestyle. Tellingly, this employee's direct replacement also left the post quickly, because senior management resolutely failed to learn from the experience of losing a valued member of staff. They never engaged with their employees, they never worked at helping these people feel involved, and they never paused to ask themselves why they had such a high turnover. This particular organisation has had a constant drain of skilled employees. What is the problem? Just like a majority of organisations today, senior management at this firm never understood the need to let go of an obsession with accounts and money. They never realised that for an organisation to be successful and profitable in the long term, it is necessary to invest money and—more importantly—time and attention in meeting the needs of valuable, valued employees.

Treating people reasonably within a management role—in other words, treating employees within a framework of customer service— is not just nice; it also makes firm management sense, and that translates to a better, more successful company.

Why? The fact is that it all comes down to emotion.

Harnessing the power of emotion

A useful way of understanding feelings and how they impact on behaviour is to place them on a scale of one to ten, with one being an unresourceful, and ten a resourceful emotion. At one, the person is feeling unresourceful: hurt, tired, depressed, disillusioned, stupid, worried, anxious, and frustrated. These unresourceful feelings do not help the employee to achieve his or her potential and do their very best. Conversely, when one's feelings are rated ten, the individual feels powerful, confident, articulate, dynamic, motivated, engaged, thrilled, loved, and supported.

A story I often tell when I am giving a seminar goes like this:

I am in Paris, and I have decided to visit the Eiffel Tower. It is the peak of the tourist season, so there is a huge queue to get in. I have been looking forward to coming for ages. In fact, seeing Paris from the top of the Eiffel Tower was a boyhood dream of mine.

"Oh well," I think when I see the queue. "I'm English, so I'm used to queuing. I might as well get in the queue."

I have been queuing for an hour and a half and I am just beginning to get near the entrance when a French tourist barges in front of me without so much as a by your leave.

"Now," I ask the people attending my course, "Given this situation, how do you think that I am feeling, on a scale of one to ten, one being an unresourceful, and ten a resourceful emotion?"

Most of the attendees of the course say that, on a scale of one to ten, I have got to be feeling about as unresourceful as it is possible to feel. I am annoyed that this guy has barged in front of me. I am angry because of his lack of manners, and I am upset that nobody seems to be prepared to do anything about it. Now, if I choose my response to this tourist's behaviour on the basis of how I am feeling, the most significant outcome will be derived from my feelings. Why was I queuing in the first place? To go up the Eiffel Tower and have a nice time, of course. The angrier I get, the more likely it is that I am not going to have a nice time at all. Reacting from my unresourceful set of emotions, what am I likely to do? Well, I could go and have a fight in my inadequate French. That would really make me cross, because not only would I be arguing with this infuriating individual, but I would not be able to make myself understood very well, either. I could push in ahead of him, and annoy everyone else in the queue. Or maybe I will just stay where I am, and quietly seethe with impotent rage. Then again, I could stomp off in fury, with no back-up plan as to what I should do for the rest of the day. Hell, it is probably too late to arrange anything anyway, so I might as well just go back to my hotel room and fume for a few hours.

Just as I am deciding which unpleasant option to take, I see the interloper climb in the lift and soar upstairs. There is no room in the lift for me, so when I finally reach the entrance, I plod all the way to the top, where I see him enjoying a cup of coffee. Ooh, now I am *really* getting cross. In fact, I am so fed up, the rest of the day has been pretty much ruined. That is it! I am not going to bother coming to Paris again.

"Why," I ask the attendees of the seminar, "Do I have to react this way? Why do I have to respond on the basis of those unresourceful emotions? What if I was able to access a whole set of resourceful emotions, and react on the basis of them instead?"

"Well, anyone would be angry in those circumstances," I am told. "Anybody would get annoyed, because the French tourist has been rude and arrogant and ignorant, and it is simply human nature to respond with anger. You are just reacting the way anybody would."

"Aha," I say. "But I have told one detail of the story wrong. The person who pushed in ahead of me in the queue was not a French tourist, but a disabled child in a wheelchair. In this circumstance, would I be annoyed?"

"Well, no, of course not. Who is going to get annoyed with a disabled child; why should they have to queue for hours?"

"But the outcome is still the same. I am still going to have to spend more time in the queue."

"But it is different."

So, what is so different? What is different is that the experience, which is essentially the same for me in both cases, is filtered through a different set of beliefs and the response is arrived at accordingly. In the second case, I am reacting from a resourceful set of emotions, because I strongly believe that it is appropriate to make way for disabled children who want to see the sights. What is different is that I do not have to react on the basis of instinctive, reactive responses. I can be rational.

Not long ago, a friend of mine provided me with an excellent real-life example of how one can choose to be rational; one that I think you will find pretty easy to relate to. Now, Ahmed had just bought a fancy new car, and he was delighted with it. That very day, he and his wife had planned to go out for a fancy meal. However, when they went outside to get into the gleaming new vehicle, there was a huge scratch right down the side of it. At this point, Ahmed could have reacted by becoming angry and upset, and ruined the whole evening. As it was, he took a deep breath and said, "Well, there's nothing we can do about it now, so let us go out and have a nice time, and we will worry about it in the morning." Off they went to enjoy their evening out. In the morning, Ahmed called the garage, which was able to repair the problem free of charge.

What happened here was that Ahmed chose to respond, rather than react, to the situation; he acted rationally, rather than emotionally. We can choose to make this decision every single time a problem or a challenge presents itself. We can choose to react on the basis of helpful, rather than unhelpful, emotions.

Understanding resourceful and unresourceful emotion

Something that does not happen nearly enough in the workplace at the current time is focusing on understanding emotion, connecting to emotion, and appreciating how emotion impacts on individuals, and how they are feeling. The Scientific Management paradigm places emphasis only on behaviour, and does not explore how the way people feel affects the way they work and live. While workers on an assembly line will also work better and feel better when they are treated with respect, an off day is less likely to have profoundly negative effects for the company than in the case of a key knowledge worker. If an employee is treated so badly they up sticks and leave, it is not a huge problem (from the point of view of management, not ethics in the workplace!) in the case of unskilled work, because another set of hands will do just as well. In the knowledge work environment, however, it is crucial to understand emotion, and how it affects the way knowledge workers feel, think and behave.

Of course, there are no objectively "bad" feelings. Any emotion can, in certain circumstances, be resourceful. For example, anger can be resourceful in certain situations, when it is right or good to be angry. Think about when a child is about to run into a busy road. It is good to be angry with the child at that time. To be angry with the child for the next three or four hours, however, is probably not very useful. Sometimes it is good to demonstrate anger to your partner, at what they have said or done, or have not said or done. But to be angry with them for the next three or four hours is not useful. The same applies in the workplace. Managers should be able to express anger when it is valid and useful, but the general atmosphere that they should try to foster at all times should be one in which workers know that they are appreciated, and are shown every day that the opportunity for them to grow and mature as workers and as individuals is being provided to them.

Whenever anyone moans to me about their job, I retort, "If you think that your work is stressful, you should try working in a call centre for a while!"

The employees of call centres deserve a huge amount of respect. Their work may not be high profile, but it calls for considerable skill and enormous reservoirs of patience and emotional intelligence. Working in a call centre is often boring and challenging at the same time; as dull as routine factory work with the added frisson of being shouted at by angry or confused costumers.. As a result, call centres typically have huge turnovers of staff as people suffer from burnout and leave. In the case of one call centre I worked with, the annual turnover was 60-80%, clearly far from ideal. Call centre work is always going to bring a certain set of difficulties with it, but adopting a customer-service attitude towards employees, and creating and maintaining a far more user-friendly work environment makes a huge difference to employee satisfaction. A good example of where they are getting it right is Invesco. Invesco's call centre incorporates a "playroom" for staff with facilities like PlayStation and a ping-pong table. Quite simply, it is a place where people can go to unwind and de-stress. Their premises include a comfortable lounge area for drinking coffee, or just relaxing, before employees have to go back into "the pit", as call centres are all-too-aptly referred to.

Clearly, one of the manager's most important objectives should be to help all of his or her employees to work from a sound basis of resourceful emotion. They will need to tend to that garden of skills, not for fear of losing their job, or because they worry about the possibility of receiving an embarrassing reprimand from the manager, but because they know that their efforts will be rewarded, and that the feel-good factor that comes from working hard and seeing the results will help them to feel better: more successful, more confident, and happier.

When managers are more connected to the emotional states of their staff, they can interpret when they are in an unresourceful or resourceful place, and they can help to shift the emotional focus to a better place. They understand that behaviours are driven by feelings, and that behaviours represent only a very small proportion of the whole person. One cannot "see" confidence, but one can see the behaviour that confidence creates. One cannot "see" disgruntlement, but one can see the behaviour that disgruntlement creates.

It is not hard to extrapolate that the emotional environment that the manager plays such a big role in creating is going to create a behavioural norm that will affect the company on every level, for good or ill. The good news is that when managers see that the behaviours they observe in their employees are not conducive to the best interests of the organisation, they can explore the underlying feelings, and work on creating an environment in which resourceful emotions will lead to an enhanced work environment and better performance.

With a resourceful set of emotions, one's behaviour is still affected on every level, but with the opposite effect, *even when the outcome of a given interaction with management is the same.* Adopting a customer-service attitude towards employees is not about giving them what they want every single time they have a request. It is about listening, understanding, and then finding a solution that will work for all concerned.

Getting personal

In order to help employees acquire resourceful emotions, managers need to engage with them on an intensely personal level. They need to leave their offices, go to where their employees are working, and ask them questions not just about their work performance, but also about their needs at home, their health, and their requirements. Of course, they also need to respect the privacy of their employees, but there should never be a situation in which they cannot ask, "How are you feeling right now?" or "Is there anything we can do to help you to meet your goals?"

We need our employees to understand that they own the power in the circle they are in.

An important element of operating a customer-service oriented workplace is recognising when it is time to make a significant change. We cannot change work environments overnight, and there will be times when no amount of attempting to be accommodating will cure a fundamental flaw in the workplace. If Kate whips around the office when someone is on a much-needed holiday, and finds that nobody is willing or able to do extra work, it is more than likely that the company is simply undermanned. Part of managing is knowing when it is time to put on an auto-responder telling clients that the company is dealing only with urgent matters right now, or when it is time to place an advertisement for that extra employee.

Training the brain; beyond flight or fight

Learning how to consistently work or manage from a basis of resourceful emotions involves literally retraining the brain, so that we are always in a position to choose, on an intellectual level, how we will react to the given set of circumstances.

Retraining the brain might sound difficult, but this is something that is well within everybody's grasp, given the willingness to explore new ways to interact with others. When one begins learning how to drive a car, one of the first things the instructor does is explain the basics of how the car's engine works. Similarly, understanding a little about how and why our brains react to things the way they do, makes retraining them a lot easier.

You have probably heard of what is referred to as the "flight or fight" response. At its most simple, this is a strong, visceral instinct that is held by almost every animal in our world. When a creature finds itself feeling threatened, it instinctively reacts in one of two ways. It runs away, or it lashes out. There is a good reason why the flight or fight response evolved, and that is to keep the organism as safe as the circumstances allow.

Human beings react to perceived danger just like all the other animals. We tend to run away, or fight back. Just like all the other animals, there are times when either fleeing or fighting is completely appropriate, of course. The problem is that we tend to bring a modified version of this powerful instinct into work with us, and find it difficult to resist its pull when we experience a problem. When we feel that our position of safety is being threatened by the situation at hand—because our manager is not happy with the way we are doing things, or because the company grapevine is talking about looming lay-offs—we often react by either "running away" from the problem, or by behaving aggressively. Either way, our behaviours are being formed on the basis of a series of unresourceful emotions rather than on rational thought, and they will do us no favours. Emotions, both positive and negative, are powerful indeed. Just think of how all-encompassing fear can be. We can be forgiven for feeling that our emotions are in charge of us, much of the time. Human beings may be toting the fanciest brains on the planet, but we are also animals with responses that are rooted not in thought, but in instinct.

The reason why our emotions are felt so strongly, and contribute so much to the way we respond to stressors in our environment, stems from our biological past. The human brain is constructed in three parts: the centre, the archipallium or R complex (also known as the "lizard" brain, because reptiles only have an archipallium), a second layer, called the limbic system and the final layer, called the neocortex.

It is deep inside the archipallium that our most deeply held instinctive responses are lodged. The human archipallium is very similar to the brains of such creatures as fish, lizards, and birds, so it will come as no surprise that it is not the seat of complex rational thought. The limbic system, shared with most other mammals, involves more sophisticated thought processes, as well as emotions such as love and empathy, but the neocortex is what takes care of complex reasoning, planning for the future, and so forth. This part of the brain is responsible for complex abstract thought, including language, mathematics, and other symbol-based thought systems. Of course, all the elements of the human brain are equally important, and instincts should not be repressed or ignored. What *does* matter is understanding why and how we feel the way we do, becoming able to differentiate between rational and instinctive responses, and then using our good old neocortex to analyse the situation, and create an environment in which unhelpful instincts are not encouraged to develop.

While there are times when running away or getting angry is the best choice to make, this is rarely if ever the case in the contemporary workplace. The problem is that nobody has told our adrenal glands.

Adrenaline is produced in the adrenal glands, which are located near the kidneys, and released into the blood stream when an emergency is perceived. Adrenaline is powerful stuff. A surge of adrenaline in the body causes smaller blood vessels to become constricted, freeing blood to the vessels in the liver and skeleton, so that they body can exert itself. At the same time, blood sugar levels rise and we experience a burst of energy as our muscles tighten and get ready for action.

What is particularly interesting, in light of the impact that our instincts have on how we react to situations in the workplace, is the fact that our brains are unable to distinguish between real and imaginary events. When we perceive a threat, we respond in much the same way, regardless of whether the threat is the fact of someone attacking us, or our fear that the company is planning a number of unannounced lay-offs, and that our name is at the top of the list. Either way, the adrenal glands go into overdrive. Part of the brain that is especially relevant to this response are the amygdalae, two clusters of neurons found in the medial temporal lobes of complex vertebrates, a category that obviously includes human beings. The amygdalae are important in processing and remembering emotional reactions. When they are stimulated, they control our emotional reactions and expressions in the face of threat or fear.

Dan Goleman refers to the role of the amygdalae in emotional reactions as the "amygdala hijack". Usually, sensations such as vision are routed through the thalamus, which directs the impulse to the relevant part of the brain, where it is processed, interpreted and understood. When the individual is in a stage of agitation, however, signals are routed through the amygdalae instead, which steers our reactions towards tried and tested responses to emotional stimuli, and releases electro-chemicals into our systems to facilitate a knee-jerk response. In the situation of having an argument with a colleague or with one's personal partner, one is responding from the amygdalae, not from the neocortex, where rational thought comes from. Everyone knows what it is like to be the victim of an amygdalae hijack. Hurt, angry, upset, or a combination of all three, our face reveals how we are feeling, and we find ourselves incapable of intelligent speech or thought. Lost for words, the best we can come up with is usually pretty lame. Afterwards, we sit and seethe, thinking of all the clever, witty comebacks we could have used, but did not. Unaware that we were briefly in the thrall of the amygdalae, we wonder why we were so tongue-tied in the first place.

You can imagine how useful instinctive responses are on the battlefield, or when facing down a lion on the savannah, but we have a problem when a stressful work environment is causing adrenalin levels to surge in the veins of employees and managers. Basically, everyone is, physiologically, all geared for a fight or to run away from the problem, and the body is programmed to tap into instinctive responses rather than intellectual ones. The emotions associated with this physiological state are so extreme that, after the stressful event, or when one is not in the stressful environment, one tends to develop belief systems about the workplace, or the people in it, that appear to justify the intensity of the emotional landscape. In turn, these belief systems give rise to a series of conditioned responses.

When we start to develop a greater level of awareness of when and how our instincts take over, we can work on developing techniques that will help us to bypass this happening at all. In order to avoid becoming victims of an amygdalae hijack, we can develop strategies that help, simple strategies such as controlling our breathing, counting slowly to ten or even leaving the room for a moment to get a glass of water and calm down. Of course, it would be far better to construct a workplace in which there is never a need for the body to switch into fight or flight mode, but even in the most equitably managed workplaces, people will sometimes get rubbed up the wrong way.

Although we humans are probably more instinctive than we would like to think, we are also happy owners of neocortices. The neocortex is the part of the brain that permits rational thought, and that makes possible a delay between a stimulus and response, and consequently, a choice as to how I am going to behave. Most animals have no rational thought at all. If you walk into a field of sheep, they will run away. If you flap your hands at a bird, it will take flight.

We can train animals to behave in certain ways by exposing them to a stimulus over and over again, and forcing a certain behaviour until, eventually, the behaviour always follows the stimulus. They are not thinking about why they are behaving in this way; they simply are. These are the techniques used by dog- or circus-trainers, who patiently repeat the desired stimulus, and force the desired behaviour, over and over again, until it has become second nature to the animal.

Like all other animals, each and every one of us has thousands of conditioned responses, but unlike other animals, we have the latent ability to identify those behaviours that are learned, and to become able to overcome them. The key to this lies not in directly focusing on the specific behaviours in question, but on the emotions that underlie them.

When we become enabled to release positive emotion and control it, the behaviours that follow will be the result of reasoned thought, and not negative, instinctive, knee-jerk reactions.

Feeling positive emotions for positive change

Just as having to work in a stressful environment sets the scene for resorting to learned responses enacted on a basis of fear and anger, a pleasant work environment fosters a situation in which one works with and from one's intellect rather than a series of unhelpful emotional responses.

Creating that positive work environment has to start with management, for it is the managers who build the emotional environment in which everybody will spend their working day.

In order for a work team and for the members of the work team to feel successful, they have got to feel the emotions that accompany success. They have got to feel needed, wanted and listened to. They have got to feel that their opinions matter and that their managers care about them, not just as workers but as individuals with needs and with medium- and long-term goals. They have got to feel that, when the time comes, they can move on from here to somewhere bigger and brighter and better. When goals are expressed to knowledge workers purely in terms of numbers—selling X amount of products, saving X amount of money, or cutting down on X amount of wastage—it is hard to identify them with emotions, especially when they are expressed in negative terms, as they so often are: "We have got to stop wasting so much money," "We are all going to have to tighten our belts," "This level of wastage is just going to have to stop!" There is not going to be the sense of excitement that accompanies doing well, knowing that one has done well, and seeing that others also know and appreciate that one has done well.

Clearly, we need to work on creating the environment within which our behaviour can change.

So, where do we start? Let us take a look, shall we?

Chapter 5)
The process of change

S o, you know that your company has to change its way of doing things, senior management has committed to the idea that it will have to look long and hard at its own assumptions and practices, you have given the pep talks, held the company-wide meetings, and set up seminars for everyone to attend. And then it is back to work! A bright new future lies ahead, right?

In business and in everyday life, change is often envisioned as an "either/ or" scenario, as if transforming oneself from one state to another was something as simple as flicking a switch. In reality, a twenty-first birthday party does not automatically confer maturity and wisdom, a new regulation does not immediately impact on public behaviour, and a company's decision to change the way it does things does not mean that this decision will be implemented at every level of the organisation or that, over time, it will be implemented in any meaningful way at all. Because humans, like all other living creatures, are intrinsically conservative—with a small c—and most comfortable performing tasks they already know how to do within parameters that are familiar to them, introducing change to an organisation, while often necessary and ultimately successful, is a difficult business that calls for honesty, patience, and space. All too often, managers decide that it is time for a new approach, without thinking through what the new circumstances will mean for the members of their organisation, and how these people will have to change their lives in order to cope with them. Instead they announce their decision to their employees, possibly arrange for a few seminars or training sessions, hold a pep talk about what a big deal it is, and then leave people to deal with it as best they can, often while doing almost nothing to change their own behaviour. All too often, the big talk is soon forgotten as everybody, management included, reverts back to the familiar approach that they have been using for years.

It is at this stage that uncertainty and doubt set in, largely because of unrealistic expectations about how quick and how easy making real, long-lasting change is going be. Having decided that changes need to be made, explored what those changes will be, and become convinced that they will be for the best, managers often find themselves aghast at the opposition and resentment they face from a surly workforce. Having already gone through the process of accepting change themselves, this can be difficult to fathom. Unless a carefully thought-out approach is put into place, actually making changes—real changes that impact on real behaviours—may take much longer than management anticipated, and unforeseen problems are likely to arise. It is now, as both managers and employees struggle with managing and implementing a new system, that old ways of doing things will be remembered with the rosy view of nostalgia; "We never had this problem until they decided we had to change things down here."

Unless management helps motivate everyone to change, the organisation is at risk of reverting back to the old ways of doing things; methods and approaches that have already been identified as less than satisfactory, but that have the dubious benefit of providing the comfort zone of the familiar.

While it can be intensely frustrating to instigate a new way of doing something, only for everyone to revert to their old habits with what seems to be impossible laziness, preventing this from happening is easier when one knows a little about *why* it happens. The fact is that behaviours that have been repeated over and over again are recorded indelibly in the very structure of our minds, becoming not just psychologically but *physically* an intrinsic element of who we are, what we do, and how we do things. Even when there is no ostensible reason to revert to a behaviour that we do not want or need to use any more, our brains will respond to given cues in our environment, and signal to us that it is time to display a tried-and-tested behavioural pattern again. This, of course, happens in every realm of existence, not just of work. Let us look at an example.

For instance, let us say you grew up in the 1980s. You were a huge fan of Sting back then, although since then your tastes have changed and now you are more of a jazz and blues enthusiast. You have not heard or even consciously thought about Sting for years but, one day when you are back in your home town visiting Mum and Dad, you find yourself wandering past the old school and you realise that, for some reason, you are singing, "I'll be watching you," under your breath. *That is odd,* you might think. *I haven't heard that song for years!* In fact, what has happened is that the action of walking past your old school—something you have not done for a while—has kicked off a behaviour that your brain associates with this action, a behaviour that is permanently recorded in your mind, so that it can be taken out and used when the moment is right.

Similarly, unless new ways of doing things are adequately implemented in the workplace, we are all likely to revert to old behaviours, given familiar cues. Habitual behaviours are stored in the basal ganglia in the brain. New behaviours can cause them to become dormant, but our minds never forget habitual behaviours, and it is easy to revert even to habitual behaviours from long ago, given the right stimulus.

As much of what we do at work is habitual, learning how to work in a different way calls for removing these cues from our environment, or becoming overtly aware of what these cues are, so that we can choose not to heed them. And of course, we also need to work at forming a new set of habitual behaviours.

In introducing changes to an organisation, it is essential to respect the process of change, and understand how the very notion of change impacts on the emotional state and, by extension, the performance of every single member of the organisation. Above, all it is essential to respect, foster, and encourage the growth of emotional intelligence in the organisation at every individual and collective level, because when the qualities that denote emotional intelligence are fostered—qualities such as empathy and motivational understanding—communicating change, identifying triggers to old behaviours and helping people to acquire new and more useful habitual behaviours is easier.

Being aware of the possible emotional reactions to change in the workplace before announcing it helps managers to cope with employees' reactions, and to plan for providing the support and training that they will need. Let us start by looking at the most common reactions amongst a workforce when a change is announced.

What to expect when you are changing

When an individual or an organisation begins a process of change, something strange happens to the way their mind works. In particular, their memory can start to play funny tricks on them. Hirshleifer and Welch describe the situation like this: "In a stable environment, the player optimally responds to memory loss with excess inertia, defined as a higher probability of following old policies than would occur under full recall." In practice, this "amnesia" makes it difficult for the individual, or the organisation's, habits to change without concerted effort over time, in an environment in which change may be talked about and proposed, but in which managerial attitudes are not actually apparent to the employee. In the face of the threat that talked-about change can seem to be, what often happens is that old ways of doing things actually become *more* entrenched rather than less, as the familiar seems to offer a comfort zone that the new just cannot. It has often been noted by psychotherapists that individuals attending therapy for one problematic behaviour or another often suffer a setback or a regression when they are nearing the end of their treatment. The individual attending therapy for overeating, for example, may have progressed well through therapy and made real progress towards identifying why he overeats, with visible results for his health and well-being. But when faced with the prospect of having neither the familiar behaviour—the over-eating—nor the therapy to fall back on, he is very vulnerable to resorting to tried and tested ways of making himself feel better in the short term, and may present himself during what should be the final sessions of therapy, having regressed to his earlier behaviour and regained some of the weight he worked so hard to lose in the first place. Helping their clients overcome this hurdle is one of the most important tasks of any therapist, but all of us are familiar with behavioural regressions from our own experience of change.

Organisational change can be prompted by the recognition that the group is performing suboptimally, or when the company must restructure for other reasons. At an individual level, it has been observed that when people face stress, they tend to adjust their beliefs to limit this stress as much as possible. In practice, this means that when they face change, they are likely to cling—not necessarily on a wholly conscious level—to the familiar and the well-known, even if these are what change is supposed to address. The same thing happens in organisations. Interestingly, the behaviours that are most well remembered and most assiduously clung to and returned to, even after an organisation announces a change of tack, are not necessarily the official policies held in the past, but the actions as they took place on the ground. In other words, managers may have been talking "pull" talk all along, but the "push" behaviour that has been modelled throughout the company is what will be remembered, and what will resist change every step of the way.

Change is rarely easy, and typically the manager who decides to implement a new approach to team meetings will be a little disappointed with the initial response, which will probably be something like, "Why are you giving me all this extra work to do? I already have to do all this stuff, and now I have to prepare a team meeting as well? What is all that about?" The new behaviour that is being displayed will arouse great suspicion, because nobody knows what is going on, and they are not sure what it will mean for them, especially if everything the manager has said and done before has suggested that he wants to be "the boss".

If the manager's role undergoes a big shift, if the manager has worked hard and succeeded in tackling the beliefs underlying his behaviour, and is displaying a new set of behaviours, it is obvious that the employees' role must undergo dramatic change too. In fact, it is probable that the first time the new format of team meeting is attempted, it will not go very well, because nobody knows what they are doing, and everybody is unsure as to how they should behave. But do you know what? That is perfectly fine, because the manager and the team are, together, embarking on a learning process. Embracing change is also about accepting the possibility that one cannot always be in absolute control of a given situation, and about accepting that this is not a problem but, instead, an opportunity for issues that are often left unaddressed to be taken on board.

The seven reactions to change

Individuals tend to experience at least one of seven different possible reactions to change when they are called into a meeting and told that, from now on, things are going to be different. Understanding what these emotions are, and how they can be expressed, makes it easier to deal with them, and helps to ease the organisation towards the new state of being that has been identified as a better one.

In my role as a management consultant, I have often been called to work for firms that are in a state of transition, and over the years I have come to recognise a number of reactions that typically emerge. I have identified these seven key reactions as follows:

1) People will feel awkward, ill and ease and self conscious.

When changes occur in someone's environment, they tend to become self-conscious and feel awkward, because they are not familiar with the new parameters, are unsure as to how they are supposed to react, and afraid that they will do something wrong. Feeling this way, they are prone to tap into a wide range of negative emotions that in turn prevent them from performing as well as they could. Coming from a basis of awkwardness and self-consciousness, they do not ask for the knowledge or information they need, avoid feeling conspicuous by keeping to themselves, and develop an over-sized fear of being ridiculed by their peers or managers, who they assume are much more au fait with the new setup than they are. These feelings are heightened when there is an inadequate supply of information to the people affected, or when management announces change without explaining why it matters, and how the changes will have to be effected.

Let us look at a simple analogy. Imagine that you go to the dentist. He peers into your mouth, and announces that a couple of teeth are going to have to be removed, and that you are going to have to have a full gum scrape, involving four more visits to the dentist so that he can clean your teeth properly. As soon as you are able to talk, you ask the dentist why the removal and gum scrape are necessary. He mutters something vague about the importance of dentistry, and tells you that your time is up, because the next client is waiting. You can pick the bill up from the receptionist on your way out.

How will you feel as you leave the dentist's surgery? You have just been told that you are going to have considerable work done on your teeth. You know that it is going to be expensive, and you are pretty sure that your health insurance package is not going to cover it. You do not particularly like visiting the dentist, and because he only works during office hours, you are going to have to rearrange your life to fit in those gum scraping appointments—and you do not even know why! I know that I would not be feeling very happy about the situation, or very optimistic about the outcome. I would probably consider changing dentist, even if my practitioner has given me good treatment so far.

If, instead, my dentist explains that by removing one tooth and eliminating a bacterial infection that is threatening my gums, I will have a much greater chance of reaching old age with all my teeth intact, I will probably feel that the intervention is worth it. After all, what is a few afternoons' inconvenience, as compared to several decades of tooth problems?

Similarly, when change within an organisation is necessary, possible ill-effects can be mitigated against by providing all the employees at every level with as much information as possible about *why* change is going to be effected, *what* the changes will involve, and *how* they will impact on the way the individuals function within the company. Armed with this information, including details of where the company is heading in the broader picture, people feel less awkward, more confident with the changes that they and their colleagues are facing, and more able to ask questions without appearing foolish. They know that things may be more difficult than usual for a little while, but they also understand that if they put in a little effort and show some patience, they will ultimately reap the reward. Honesty is key. Avoid saying something like, "We are going to have a lot of fun shaking things up around here!" unless you are sure that this is true. Say, "Now, making these changes is going to be a little stressful, and we are all going to reach Friday evening feeling pretty worn out for a couple of months, but we are expecting them to translate into real benefits for everyone very quickly, and we are here to help you through them."

2) People will worry about what they are being asked to give up

Instinctively, many people's first reaction to change is to ponder all the things that they will have to relinquish, or think they will have to relinquish. The familiar may not be working as well as it should, but it at least has the virtue of being easy to navigate. Maybe the organisation is not doing as well as it could, but at least everybody knows where they stand in relation to everybody else.

Companies often instigate change because they are not doing as well as they should or could. Change is often presented to the workers as a series of unpleasant cutbacks that are vital to the organisation's survival, and management braces itself for having to fight it out with the employees, rather than for useful, constructive dialogue. Typically, if the company says, "We are changing the terms and conditions around your pay structure," employees will respond by saying, "What are you taking away from me now?"

Although the impression employees receive is that change is invariably about cutbacks, losses and demotions, the truth is that managers invariably instigate change in an attempt to make things *better* for everyone in the company, not worse! Of course, changes do sometimes involve cutbacks, but the cutbacks are not the point of the exercise; the improved cash-flow, or better working conditions after the cutbacks, are what it is all about.

In the 1970s, Ford car manufacturing employed almost 35,000 people in the United Kingdom. Almost overnight, it was announced that half of these people were going to lose their jobs. The response, as you can imagine, was one of dismay and chaos as the workers and unions reacted with horror. What one heard on the news every single day was that Ford was axing 17,500 jobs, with the implication that Ford managers were callous individuals, who were out to make as many people miserable as possible. Less obvious than the fact that half of the workforce was going to go, was something more important; Ford was acting so as to *save* 17,500 jobs. It was facing a crisis situation, and continuing with a massive 35,000 workforce meant certain closure, and twice as many people out of a job. In the 1970s, car manufacturing was undergoing mechanisation. If Ford had resisted the trend, it would soon have lost out to its more innovative competitors.

When changes are necessary, it is essential that management explain the rationale behind the changes, and especially explain the positives behind them. It is true that change is not always easy—that, in fact, it is often painfully difficult—but when everyone understands why it is necessary, and how the company and its workers will benefit as a result, it is easier. It is also essential to allow members of the company time to process the new information, and space to give out about it! Viewed from the comfort-zone of a set of resourceful emotions, the inevitable complaints that emerge when impending change is announced can be seen as an opportunity to communicate with employees, and even learn from their views about what potential drawbacks to the new circumstances will be. Managers who face initial resistance should never see this as a personal attack, or indicative of employee disloyalty, but as what it really is; an invitation to dialogue.

3) People will feel alone, even if everyone is going through change at the same time.

Do you remember your first day at school? Your mother probably brought you there to give you support, and you probably clung to her hand for as long as you possibly could before going in that door. The fact that twenty of your future classmates were starting their first day of school at exactly the same time, and that all over the country tens of thousands of five-year-olds were also finding it hard to let go of mummy's hand, did nothing to lessen your feeling of being alone in the big, bad world for the first time.

We all get used to change, but something that remains constant is the fact that we all feel alone when we are going through the process of change, regardless of how many people are actually accompanying us on that journey. Feeling isolated, we also feel responsible for carrying the burden of our solitude, and the longer we feel alone, the more we suffer from the sensation that nobody knows, understands, or cares about what is going on in our lives. This is not a pleasant feeling, and as the weight we have to shoulder seems to get heavier and heavier, we tend to crawl deeper and deeper inside our shell, making our burden all the heavier to bear in the process.

To avoid this scenario taking place, it is important to get as much of the team involved as possible, because when we pull together as a team it is much easier to accept change. People need to know that they are not really alone, that help is there when they need it, and that they are free to express anxieties and reservations without having to worry about facing recrimination.

4) People can only handle so much change at once.

Nobody can cope with everything in their environment changing all at once and no manager can expect his employees to be able to completely transform the way they do things without so much as the blink of an eye. An old saying goes: "You cannot swallow an elephant whole, but you can swallow it in bite-size mouthfuls," and we do well to remember it.

Different people can handle different amounts of change at any one time. Change is a dynamic process, of course, but it is vital that employees be allowed to change at their own pace, without forcing those involved to take on more than they can handle at any one time. As new ways of doing things are instigated, managers will need to remain very close to the prevailing mood, and gauge the pace of change. Timing is everything.

5) People are ready to change in varying degrees.

People have different attitudes towards change. Some love the exciting environment it creates, while others feel threatened, and tend to resist change as much as they can. Neither approach is better than the other. The change-lovers can risk throwing the baby out with the bathwater, while change-haters can resist doing things in a new, more effective way. Key to dealing with different peoples' needs is understanding that everyone has a unique reaction to changes in their environment. Managers need to make change easier for their whole team, by making sure that they understand what it means to the people within it, and how they can each be helped, as individuals, to take on board the new ways of doing things. Often, those who protest the hardest have the easiest time getting on with things, because they take time to think through potential difficulties and, if they are given the support they need, can find solutions.

6) People will be concerned that they do not have enough resources.

A common response is that the changes posited are fine, but that there are insufficient resources to cope with them. "Sure," the individual will say. "I don't mind doing X, Y and Z, but I will need more time, money and co-workers."

While some changes will need more material resources, others do not, and it is the manager's job to provide information about what resources are available. They must also help to provide with the resources currently available within the organisation, such as the manager's own expertise, the capacity of the team to work as a closer unit, and so forth.

The team ethos as a resource is a very powerful force, as well as the fundamental ability of the human spirit to discover new and better approaches. People underestimate the resources they have within, especially the power of the human mind, once deployed efficiently.

7) If the pressure is removed, people will revert back to old behaviours.

Typically, managers are good about announcing change and beginning to implement it, but fall very far short when it comes to following change through to the desired conclusion. They present their team with a new way of doing things, state that this is what they expect from now on, and then leave people to get on with things. Without support and a little pushing, we all tend to revert to behaviours and systems that we are already familiar with, because—in the short term, at least—this is easier, and we feel comfortable doing what we already know. Besides, unless work is done on changing the belief system that underlies the old behaviours, a reversion will be inevitable. During a transition phase, with all the uncertainty about the future that prevails, the tendency to cling to old ways of doing things will be strong. Beliefs, however, can and will change over time, so long as managers model behaviours to support the new beliefs, allow positive experiences connected to the new beliefs to accumulate, and resist attempts to revert to the old ways of doing things.

It is vital that people experience the effects of change as beneficial, because if change is experienced as unpleasant for a prolonged period, it will not become intrinsic to the culture of the organisation which is, of course, something that must happen if the changes are to make any substantive difference to the way that things are done.

Our solution to the challenges embodied in creating and maintaining change is the Votive Process, a process that focuses on exploring and understanding how learning occurs, and then supporting that process through to its conclusion, which is a series of fully integrated, new ways of behaving adapted to the organisation's real aims and aspirations.

The nature of learning; the importance of repetition

People remember things they have done much better than they remember things they have heard and seen. Why? Well, when someone does something, they see for themselves what the outcome of the action is. When they do something over and over again, they see it over and over again, until the action has become an integrated part of their behaviour. Memory, including the memory of how to do something, is also prompted by associations. Doing specific things, or consistently approaching tasks in a specific way, will create more and stronger associations than just sitting in a seminar room listening to somebody talk. For instance, to look at a simple example of how doing something repeatedly creates associations, let us assume that a friend of yours once recommended a particular brand of biscuits as especially delicious. You remember his advice the next time you go to the supermarket, and pick a packet off the shelf. At home, you find that—yum!—they really *are* delicious. You buy them the next time you go shopping too, and then every other time, until reaching out for that particular brand has become part of your regular shopping routine. By the time a few months have passed, you probably do not remember why you started buying those particular biscuits in the first place, but the repeated actions of buying, eating with pleasure, and buying again are instantly recalled every time you go into a supermarket and they influence your behaviour—you reach for that beloved packet every time you shop until or unless something (a diet, perhaps!) changes this behaviour.

By consciously utilising repetition in the learning, changing environment, we can forge new habitual behaviours to replace the old ones that are no longer valid.

As Hirshleifer and Welch say: "Organisational action requires arousal and attention by coordinating individuals. When an action is taken and repeated, it leads to effects, and these effects provide repeated reminders of what the action was that led to these effects. Actions are therefore salient, and involve a richness of arousal, associations and rehearsal."

In order to create an environment in which new behaviours can be learned, we need to create an environment that is different to the old one, because everything that remains the same is rich with associations with how things used to be.

Change is all about learning, and key to the learning process is repetition. With the exception of instinctive actions, as we discussed above, every single thing we know—how to get dressed, how to eat with chopsticks, how to read, how to interpret a flow chart, how to use the Internet—was learned. For every skill we have mastered, there are, of course, millions we have not. Not knowing how to do something does not mean that we will never know how to do it. It means that we have not yet learned. If we are properly taught or self-taught, we can acquire the new knowledge and skills we need. Our abilities are limited, but our aptitudes are countless.

Children and adults alike do not acquire new skills immediately, but through a process of learning that does not take place on just one level. If you want to learn Spanish, for example, you will not start by tackling Don Quixote, but by learning how to say, "hello" and "goodbye." Even those two small words might be difficult for a little while, and you might feel embarrassed when you start using them in public, but by repeating them over and over, and learning how to use them in context, they will soon become second nature. Little by little, your vocabulary will be augmented and, as you repeat the task of using your new words in an appropriate context, they will become engraved on your memory.

This gives us the first rule of learning: it is an incremental process that involves much repetition.

In order to teach it is, of course, essential that those who are being taught are receptive to the teacher's message. They need to be in a situation in which they are able to concentrate, and any theoretical or practical opposition they might have to the lesson should be dealt with. In other words, in the context of a company, employees should understand why they are being asked to master a new skill or set of skills. Only then will the manager's words penetrate and become integrated into a new set of beliefs and behaviours.

Repetition when learning is not just about practice making perfect, because repetition actually makes possible the creation of new connections— synapses—between the neurons in our brains. These connections are what make acquiring and implementing new skills possible. It is true that children's brains are wired to acquire new information more quickly, but learning is something that can take place at any period in the individual's life.

The human brain is composed of tissues that contain neurons, synapses, and chemicals. The neuron is like the wire that connects your computer or router to the Internet; it transmits information back and forth. The network of neurons that extends all over the brain allows different sections of the brain to communicate with each other. At the end of each neuron there are extensions called "dendrites", with gaps between them connected by small electrical charges that bridge the synapse, carrying information with them. When babies are born, their untested brains have many more neurons than an adult's, but few synapses, because they have great capacity to learn, but have had very few actual learning experiences. In childhood and adulthood, the physical process of learning is the same. With each new experience, the brain experiences activity in a particular neural pathway. Each time the experience is repeated, the electrical signal becomes stronger until, eventually, it has become a pattern of signals that the brain automatically recognises, making information easier to process.

The manager who would like to see real, meaningful change occur in his or her organisation is one who facilitates this natural process of learning, by making it possible for employees not only to encounter new ways of doing things, but to practice them until the new approach has been literally wired into the hardware of their minds.

The manager who oversees change has to stop thinking of him or herself as someone who makes decisions, tells people about them, and then makes sure that they are implemented. Effective managers overseeing change become mentors who help their employees through every step of the process of change, while accepting that they, too, will have to alter the way they work and think. It is not enough to arrange a training session or a leadership exercise or to send bulk emails now and again, reminding everyone of the new policy. The manager's job is to think about what change means for the people involved, how it will impact on the way they work, which aspects of change are difficult and how each and every member of the organisation will have to be assisted in integrating the desired changes into his set of behaviours. The manager will have to be prepared to start a learning process that will involve a lot of hands-on communication and repetition, not just of words and instructions, but of the new behaviours that will effect the desired changes, and also help in the formation of a new belief system that will support those changes.

Currently, what happens far too often is that, when a company decides to introduce a new way of doing things, it "does" or "provides" a training course—*once*—and then expects employees to be able to implement the new approach. Why? We do not expect the new student of Spanish to be able to master the language after just one class, and who would sit their driving test after just ten minutes behind the wheel? Learning new skills in the workplace is no different. *Hearing* information is not the same as *understanding* it, understanding it is not the same as being able to *implement* it, and implementing it once is certainly not the same as *integrating* it into one's set of everyday behaviours, until it has become second nature. Remember those synapses? They need time and practice to form.

Effective training programs include sessions where attendees practice and repeat their new skills, and receive feedback from their managers, or the facilitators running the course. Feedback is crucial during training and subsequently, because it is only through feedback that employees learn when they are doing things well, and when not so well. It goes without saying that positive reinforcement is infinitely more useful than negative. Telling people when they are doing something well, and explaining how and why their good performance benefits the organisation, is essential.

Of course, there is always a risk that, over time, people will relapse to their old behaviour. Fortunately, steps can be taken to minimise this risk, and counter it when it does occur. Ideally, relapses to older behaviours are taken as examples to talk about how and why the old behaviour is less effective, and to find an approach within the new paradigm that will work better.

One of the clients I have worked with is insurance provider, Eaglestar. Eaglestar is an established provider with a good record in its field, and when Eaglestar's senior managers decided to integrate a new performance management system, they realised that they would need a change of management culture to make it work. Now, the system itself was not particularly complicated. The idea was to link performance management much more closely with performance development. Moving management away from appraisal and towards development was about moving it towards a twelve-month program, with views set firmly on the horizon, rather than keeping an eye on daily minutiae. Successfully making the shift called for a change in the culture of management, and this could only happen if everyone in the organisation learned how to behave and how to think about their organisation in a completely different way. The first step was to hold a series of workshops about employee involvement with the new system, so that everybody could think and talk about what was important. The guiding principles that emerged from these workshops were preparation, participation, honesty, and continual process; no surprises there. But, as we know, the trick lies not in knowing how to manage, but in actually believing in what you say and implementing it.

The first stage that Eaglestar set up was a series of workshops towards creating what management felt would make a good performance development system. These led to a further series of workshops for all those people who had line management appraisal responsibility. At the second series of workshops, the focus was on discussing the principles that had been set, from a practical point of view. What would these principles look like in practice? How could they be worked into the new approach? In other words, each unit within the organisation created its own individual action plan as to how they were going to make the changes that needed to be made. Over the course of the next six weeks, the workshops were followed up with a series of audiofile and PDF files provided to employees that reinforced the message, effectively reproducing it in different formats and presenting it to members of the organisation: repetition, repetition, repetition! Simultaneously, a mentoring process was instigated. Work was monitored, and employees were encouraged to share experiences of the new system, and support each other in using it. A few months later, a further series of meetings was held, so that everyone could discuss the success of the implementation of the new approach, and brainstorm around ideas to make it work even more smoothly.

What the people at Eaglestar had understood, and what they integrated into their approach to adopting a new technique, is that accepting change, moving with it and reaching a new plateau of ability, is all about learning, and learning in adulthood is not substantially different to any learning that takes place earlier in life. The child who is being taught how to read is undergoing a process of change and, just like the adult who is going through a process of change, all the benefits that she will reap as a result of acquiring the new skill are accompanied by loss. The increased independence that literacy will bring will be accompanied by the increased need to answer for her own judgements, for example. Fortunately, as children we do not worry too much about why we are learning; we just do it.

The steps of learning

Again, in adulthood as in childhood, learning is not a process that takes place quickly, but in incremental steps. The first stage in the process is **unconscious incompetence**, also known more colloquially as "ignorant bliss", when one does not know that one cannot do something. This state is exemplified by the child perched on Daddy's knee who is allowed to steer the car across the field, not realising for a moment that he is not really driving.

This stage is succeeded by **conscious incompetence**, when one knows that one cannot do something. For example, you might be very competent at using the Microsoft Word© program that is installed on your computer, but you know that you have not yet tackled the graphics programs that would enable you to manipulate digital images. You have the computer, you have the software, you know that there is a manual somewhere on the hard drive, and you expect that, given the time you require, you would probably be able to master it. At the same time, you realise perfectly well that if called upon today, you would not be able to use the program. At this stage, the decision to do what it takes to acquire the new information or skill can be made. "I will skip watching the match tonight," you can think, "and get to grips with this software program instead."

From this level, one moves to being **consciously competent.** The individual *knows* that they can do something, but they do not *feel* completely confident about their abilities. When they attempt the new task, they feel anxious and nervous. They are afraid they will screw up, and worry that they will be exposed to ridicule if they do. Remember how you felt the day you took your driving test? That is pretty much what conscious competence feels like. Every gesture, every decision you make is accompanied by self-doubt and the worried thought, "Am I doing this wrong?"

Little by little, of course, those feelings of anxiety and doubt dissipate as the skill is mastered, and finally the stage of **unconscious competence** is reached, when the formerly new skill or knowledge has been assimilated, and there is no longer any need to think about it.

Every learning process follows the same trajectory, and acquiring and implementing new ways of managing are really no different, so if you find yourself contemplating change with anxiety, or beginning to implement change and realising that you are not getting everything right all of the time, do not worry, because all that this means is that you are a perfectly normal human being. The same goes for each and every member of the community that is your organisation.

Change begins with learning how to learn

Over the course of our lives, we all acquire presuppositions. Some of these are useful, but others are counterproductive, and can prevent us from achieving all that we would like to. We grow accustomed to assuming that things are "just so" when, in fact, they could just as easily be another way. We tend not to change our ways of thinking, because they have become so very ingrained. Just as the manager usually assumes, "I run the team meeting!" the staff have acquired the habit of thinking, "Team meetings? Well, the manager runs the team meeting and we sit here and listen, chip in, and then go away. Sometimes, when he is really boring, we just try to keep our eyes open and look as though we are listening..."

It is not difficult to understand how habitual thinking can be damaging. But changing habitual thinking is not easy, and it calls for patience and insight. Before habitual thinking can be altered, we all need to work on raising our awareness of what we think, and why and how we think that way. We have to enable ourselves to switch off the autopilot that has been allowing us to bumble along. We have got to embrace conscious incompetence, becoming unafraid to admit, "I can do it, but I am going to be crap at it." At that stage, we can have that ineffective team meeting in a new format but, more importantly, we have started the process of becoming able to do things in a different way. We are also modelling to our employees that doing something new is feasible. It might be awkward, it might be a little rough around the edges, but it is worth trying because, with practice, it will be much better.

Even after that first awkward new-format meeting, there are hurdles that may affect the way things continue to develop. First and foremost, it is not unlikely that everyone at the meeting is going to come down with a serious case of what I call "excusitis"—really just a series of excuses as to why we are not changing, and why we are already deciding to abandon all those fine decisions about a new way of doing things. We say, "It is just not me," "I just cannot do it," "I am just not one of those people," and of course, the classic, "I did it and it did not work, so I am not going to make that mistake again!"

What we need to do, when we really wish to learn, is succeed in breaking through conscious competence. We have to be prepared to put in time and effort to create a new set of habits. We have to be prepared to learn. We have to give our new habits the time and space they need to grow, if we are determined not to let our old habits return. If you do not believe me, ask anyone who has been through the painful struggle of giving up smoking!

The nature of change

Although effective change is always about a transformation in the underlying belief systems of a company, currently the focus is always on the surface changes: cost-cutting, improvements in performance, restructuring, or dealing with a crisis. In the aftermath of the change, managers tend to judge the success or otherwise of what has been done by comparing "before" and "after" figures. Doing this a short time after the change has been instigated is, however, of limited use, because it is still far from unlikely that the company will revert, over time, to its old model of doing things. More useful, in the longer term, is looking at how the changes affect the company's development, growth and performance over a sustained period, rather than in the weeks or months after change has been announced. Frequently, before and after pictures taken not long after the change paint quite a rosy picture, while a little further down the road, this is just not the case. Again, this trend is not just seen in company spreadsheets. We have all seen before and after pictures of people who have undergone massive weight loss. But how often are we shown an "after" picture of the same person several years after the crash diet? Long term results are infinitely more important than short-term when we are talking about the dieter keeping the pounds off, or the company raking them in!

In a 2006 survey, the McKensie Quarterly reported that many companies— about a third of those surveyed—reported only partial success in achieving change, while ten per cent reported absolute or near failure in achieving any of the goals they had set themselves. When they looked at the business reporting relatively high levels of success (38%) in achieving change, they all had one thing in common: communication. In the words of the report: "A majority of all [successful] respondents say their organization sought to define clear goals for the next one to two years and communicated the transformation as a compelling story, and a little under half say that their company offered an inspiring view of a better long-term future."

Now that is very revealing. The companies that succeeding in effecting change *told* their employees what was going on, and *showed* them how the changes that were about to take place would reap benefits in the middle to long term. In other words, they involved them in the process of change, gave them the time and space they needed to learn a new set of beliefs and associated behaviours, and modelled the sort of behaviour that would support the new beliefs that they sought to encourage. The report also stated that: "Respondents with the most successful transformations reckon that their company was conspicuously more effective than the others at raising expectations about future performance, addressing short-term performance, engaging people at all levels of the organization, including a clear and coordinated program design, and making the change visible— through, say, new IT tools or physical surroundings."

Above all, the companies surveyed by the McKensie Quarterly that succeeded in changing recognised and dealt with the fact that emotions were key to performance transformation, especially the fostering of useful resourceful emotions, such as a sense of focus and enthusiasm.

Too often, companies dealing with transition focus on employees "resistance" to change, and categorise the organisation's workers as problems that have to be dealt with, rather than as key players within the organisation, who are valued assets and important people, whose feelings about the change have to be respected. Any fears and trepidation about the future are dismissed, are not discussed with the attention they deserve, or are seen as overt threats to the status quo and greeted with aggression. None of these approaches is remotely useful. Employees are right to be concerned. Change *is* difficult. Some of them might have to go. Some may have to put in longer hours until the transition has been completed. Everything that happens to them at work will impact on the way they live outside work, on their families, loved ones, and place in society. If the company call centre moves from Manchester to Newcastle, how many families will have to uproot themselves? Often, it is not just the change per se that causes alarm, but the thought of going through the process of change, and all the extra physical and emotional effort that will be expended as they struggle to find their place in the context of a rapidly shifting work environment. Consequently, while it is vital to outline why the company has to move away from point A and towards point B, and essential to explain what is so hot about point B, it is also necessary to look at all the steps that each and every employee will have to take along the way, and explain exactly why each step matters, and how management will support every single member of the organisation on their personal journey towards where they need to be, when everyone gets to point B. What is more, information on these changes should come directly from management, face-to-face with the employees, with time and space provided to deal with questions and uncertainties. An organisation's workers deserve not to hear about major changes on the company grapevine, by means of a bulk email, or over the company intercom. Managers must never forget that workers should understand exactly how and why the change will benefit them, because without this knowledge their motivation to change will simply not be there. Organisations where an atmosphere of trust, openness, and emotional support prevails invariably find change easier and less stressful.

Avoiding failure/avoiding success

One of the biggest barriers to the successful integration of a new way of doing things is the avoidance of failure and its flipside, success avoidance.

The one thing that most adults avoid as much as possible is failure. Most adults cannot bear to be seen to fail, so they have developed failure avoidance strategies that make failure, or at least public failure, impossible.

For instance, over the years I have learned that the majority of attendees at a training session will sit as close to the back of the room as they can, just like kids on a school tour bus. They will feel quietly pleased if they manage to grab a seat in the back row, invariably the row that is filled first. It is very likely they will not be able to see the visual aides or the speaker back there, and they may not be able to hear him very well, either. Sitting in the back row is hardly the logical choice to make.

So why on Earth *do* they want to sit in the back row?

The bottom line is that they are afraid of being seen to fail. They are afraid that if they sit near the front, they might be asked a question, and if they do not know the answer, everyone might laugh at them, and then they will feel like even more of a failure. They are afraid that their companions will think that they are losers, and that they will not be liked. They might not be able to admit to these feelings, because when you say it straight, it really does sound pretty silly, but they feel them anyway, because feeling this way is something that we are all familiar with.

The fear of failure probably starts in what psychologists refer to as the latency period. The term "latency period" was originally coined by Sigmund Freud as denoting the period between the age of about six and adolescence, when the libido appears to be repressed, and when the child's experiences are dominated by the act of learning what it is to be a member of society, both in the context of formal education and in observing those around him. In early childhood, our minds are open to any new experience, but when people reach the age of six or so, they become intensely aware of those around them and of their place in the world. Anything that happens in the course of childhood, and especially during the latency period, continues to reverberate throughout each person's experience of adulthood. This is when children start to be afraid of seeming different to their peers, or of inviting criticism or ridicule if they do something wrong in front of their parents or other authority figures. During this period, we develop coping strategies to avoid making ourselves vulnerable to stress. Typically, these strategies include avoiding failure at all cost, even at our *own* cost, because while going out on a limb can seem to invite failure, it is also necessary to achieve success. The fears and anxieties that take root in individuals during the latency period invariably continue to be present in adulthood.

The curious thing is that failure avoidance and success avoidance are really the same thing. By being afraid of accepting the possibility of failing the first few times we try something, we seriously hamper our chances of succeeding. In the example I gave above, attendees are upping their chance of failing by huddling at the back of the room, where they will not be able to hear or see what is going on. They are not only avoiding the possibility that they might look a little foolish in front of their companions; they are also avoiding being in the right place at the right time to hear the right message.

This curious avoidance of failure and success is a counterproductive habit that is acquired with time. Imagine how far humanity would have progressed, if we were born with it! Anyone who has ever spent time with a child will have seen at first hand how quickly small children learn. The reason why is that they have not yet acquired the notion that they should avoid the possibility of failure. Instinctively, they know that they have to try things over and over again to master them, even if that means getting it wrong plenty of times before the given task is accomplished.

What would happen if small children thought the way adults did? Little Peter would be crawling around, when it occurs to him that maybe he will try standing up and walking. After all, his parents seem to find it useful. So Peter stands up and—of course—he falls down straight away. He stands up again, and again he falls down. Finally, he says to himself, "Stuff this for a lark. Clearly, I am not a standing up sort of guy. I will just stick with crawling from now on." Peter's friend Paul is even less adventurous. He has been sitting in the corner all this time, watching Peter standing up and falling, and thinking to himself, "Well, if you ask me, I do not think that this standing business is all it is supposed to be. Look at him! He tried it—several times, too—and he just fell over and hurt himself. Well, I am not going to be so foolish! No way. That is far too scary for me. There is no way you will see me trying that standing lark!"

The emotions that I feel, the set of resourceful or unresourceful emotions that result from those feelings, these are the factors that create my outcomes. These are the factors that contribute to failure and success avoidance. What we need to do is raise our awareness of the emotions that we are experiencing, and take greater responsibility for them. The more responsibility we take for ourselves and what we do, the easier it becomes to tap into powerful emotions of competence, success, and satisfaction. The easier it will become to take personal responsibility for how we are feeling. When we are happy, we know that it is because we have worked hard and well to reach the given situation. When we are not, we know that it is in our power to turn things around. Either way, it is good.

So yes, change can be difficult. But that is not a bad thing. In fact, accepting that it is difficult is the first step towards effecting it. In organisations, change has to begin with senior management, who are the individuals who lead the workforce by example and who set the tone for not just change, but the way in which the company operates, every single day. These are the people who will have to be persistent in avoiding reversion back to old ways of doing things. Key to successful implementation of change is for everyone to understand why change is necessary, and to become inured to the idea that to try something new is to invite failure. With time, repetition and patience, new ways of doing things will become second nature.

Chapter 6)

Creating vision

Forging change—positive, useful change—begins with knowing where one wants to go as a company, as teams within a company and as individuals within those teams, and in understanding what values one wishes to propagate within the organisation, and display to the wider world. This knowledge is what we call "vision" which, as you will probably know, is one of the most abused and misunderstood words in the lexicon of business writing. It is also one that is worth reclaiming from the morass of talk without focus about how businesses should be run.

Why?

The fact is that a clear vision, accompanied by a strategy and the will to engage with each of the organisation's members, is a blueprint for success, and it is something worth investing time and money in, not just once, but every day.

Creating vision

No matter what sort of company one works in, the term "vision" will be familiar. Somewhere along the way, a mission statement will have been written and adopted as the company's much-vaunted "vision". It will have been printed out, laminated, and distributed and, after a while, stuck at the back of most of the employees' drawers and promptly forgotten because nobody, with the possible exception of senior management, thinks that it has any relevance to the way they work on a daily basis. The way the majority of organisations are run, this assessment is correct. Employees know that they are expected to come into work on time, do their thing without making too many mistakes, and go home. That is the message that they are receiving from their managers every single day, if not explicitly, then in the way they are spoken to and listened to, and in terms of what they are told to prioritise. Most employees are told that they have to work well without incurring unnecessary expenses, to produce on time, and to make sure the company shows a profit. Few are told or shown on a regular basis that their goal is to be true to the organisation's vision.

It is easy to have vision when you are on the board of management, but it is also easy to forget that *everyone* has to have vision at the level at which they are working. Everybody has to have a reason to come to work and give it all they have got, beyond the simple motive of wanting and needing that monthly pay-cheque.

We have already discussed how much self-identity comes from what we do. Feeling good about ourselves springs from feeling good about what we do and where we do it, and that is an integral part of having vision on an individual level. The fresh-from-A-levels junior assistant has to have a vision. The manager of the call centre has to have a vision. The manager of the company canteen has to have a vision. The head of the board of directors has to have a vision. It is easy to understand why senior management has to have a vision, but maybe not quite so straightforward appreciating why this is just as important among the secretaries, assistant clerks, and other such people, whose aspirations and desires are so often ignored in organisations, just as nineteenth century line workers' aspirations and desires were out of the picture back when Scientific Management was developed.

So why *do* the visions of all these people matter?

Quite simply, without a vision, there is no incentive to work well and there is no incentive to invest emotionally in an organisation as a place in which to grow, develop, and become self-realised in a way that makes us feel proud and good about ourselves. Without vision, we are all put-upon line workers, putting in the hours between starting work and punching out and going home; a scenario that creates a management/employee dichotomy at work that is destructive on both an individual and an organisational level. Instead, we all need to know what we are working towards, and why and how our work is going to benefit us in the medium and long term. Senior management typically spends a lot of time fretting over their vision, and whether they know where they are going or not, but when you go to talk to that call centre manager and say, "So, John, what's your vision?" the odds are that John will look at you blankly: "Eh? Vision? I am just keeping the call centre ticking over; I am nobody important. What do *I* need to have a vision for?"

John might not be the highest flyer in the company (although it is foolish to underestimate anybody's potential), but the work he does is absolutely crucial for everything to continue functioning well. John's job is important, and it is important not just for him, but for the whole organisation, that he is happy and fulfilled at work, and committed to both nurturing his garden of skills, and contributing to the continued growth and well-being of the organisation. The same goes for Kate in the canteen and James in the mail room. Yet, almost always, people like John and Kate and James are ignored or glossed over when it comes to getting members of an organisation emotionally and practically involved in creating and fostering vision. They are being sold short and, at the same time, so is the organisation.

In the process of creating effective management, it is vital for vision to be created at all levels of local management, and at its most basic that vision should answer the questions:

❖ What is going to make me come to work and be successful?

❖ What is that going to look like?

❖ What is it going to feel like?

❖ What will make me feel good about myself and what I do, and inclined to keep striving towards more of the same?

Vision should not just be about helping the company to make the money it needs to make, and have the turnover the bosses demand, but about how each of its employees functions within it, and how they feel in that function in the context of a living, dynamic organisation. It should be about employees not just as cogs in the wheel but as living, breathing human beings, whose aspirations, goals and hopes need to realised at work, just as they do at home, and at play. It is about integrating individual and team vision with that of the organisation, until they are melded together inseparably.

First creation/second creation

In order to understand vision on a holistic, complete level, managers will need to tune in much more to their creative side. It is essential to understand that creation—whether we are talking about a product or a service—is something that happens twice. A chair, a shirt, a car, a unique service; whatever it is, is created once, when the individual or the team conceives of it for the first time, and a second time, when it is physically made or physically provided. Before a chair can be built, someone has to sit down and think about what the finished product will look like. Only then can the chair be made. Similarly, before a building is physically built, someone has to sit down and decide what the building is going to look like. The architect has to visualise where everything will be, what shape the rooms will be, where the windows and doors will go, and so on. The architect's mind envisions everything, and filters these visions through his previous experience—his training at university, work he has done before—arriving finally at a plan, a vision, for the completed house.

What every manager wants is the success of his or her business and, as with any project, creating success in business begins with the first creation, with envisioning what that success will look like and feel like, and then communicating this mental creation to all the members of the organisation, and showing them where and why what they do matters.

So think: What will success look, feel, and sound like? What will be the paradigm by which you will judge success? How will you know when your work is bringing real dividends to you and your organisation? What about the guy in the call centre, or that new girl who does the photocopying? How will *they* know? What will motivate them to improve their performance, hone their skills, and start to care about their organisation and their future in it? What, in other words, will help them to make their personal vision an integral part of the vision of the organisation?

Every action we take, whether at home or at work, is composed of three qualities; knowledge, action, and being. None of the three is more important than any other. Certainly, knowledge, the first creation activity, is critical, but you have to know how to apply it and live it.

In the context of performance management, it is crucial for the individual to define what success will look like. Once this visioning process is complete, it will be easy to identify what needs to be done, in order to create that success. This process should be encouraged at every level of the organisation, as each individual within the group should "vision' both performance management and performance development success in relation to themselves. When I say "every level", I really mean it. I am not talking about every level—oh, except for those lowly new recruits in the bottom rungs, whose opinions do not matter very much. Everyone's opinions are valid and important.

Yes, creating vision should include the wisdom and insight of all the members of a work community, from senior management to the youngest, newest, most wet-behind-the-ears person on the shop floor. Years of experience build knowledge and wisdom, but they also make it much more difficult to see things objectively, while neophytes can bring an astonishing clarity to their interpretations of any given scenario. All results then need to be shared with management.

Traditionally, performance management involves ensuring, on an ongoing basis, that team and organisation goals are being met effectively and efficiently. Performance development focuses on ensuring that everyone knows what is expected of them, and can work with the time management procedures necessary to complete everything in a focused way. Ideally, performance management gives employees the forum they need to ask for feedback about their work, request help in areas they are finding difficult, and look for reinforcement in areas they are performing well in. The problem is that, historically, performance management has been seen as a paper-filling exercise, because the support has not been there when it came down to it, and people have not been given the space they need to say, "Can you help me out here? I am finding activity X quite difficult, and I need some input from you." This absence of support confirms to members of an organisation that, while management may say a lot of fine words about it, they do not really care that much about following through. This in turn will support the pervasive belief that there is little point in bothering with what are thought to be useless exercises.

True leadership involves following up what happens after the first creation has taken place. If management is about first creation, process is about doing everything that needs to be done to make the vision reality. If our vision calls for changes within the organisation, we will need to begin and consistently apply processes that create and foster emotional learning, and buy into understanding emotional intelligence as a crucial asset. We may also have to invest in development, new infrastructure, and training, but none of this will be enough if it is not applied with vision, application, and intelligence.

Knowing, doing, being

Let us look at an example: Two children are in a supermarket, helping Mum with the shopping. One kicks the other and he starts to cry. Mother turns around and says, "Say sorry!" and he growls, "Sorry." He knows he has got to be sorry, he has said sorry, but is he *being* sorry? Absolutely not, and his sibling knows it.

In the workplace, managers have generally studied teamwork, and carried out teamwork exercises, and are always ready to say a few words about the importance of working as a team. But what really matters is not what they *say*, but how they *behave*, and who they are *being*, because their behaviour—their means of being—reveals what they really feel. Do they sit at the head of the table? Do they see themselves as "the boss"? Do they say "I know best" with their actions, while giving lip service to the notion of sharing?

An equation that I often find myself quoting, because it speaks of something that we all do well to remember, is $E + R = O$. In other words, the experience plus the response equals outcome. Outcome is determined by how we choose to respond to the things that happen to us.

Everything we do has three qualities, the three qualities of knowledge. In creating, we need to *know* things. We need to know where we are, and where we would like to be going. We need to know what technical skills we require to complete the tasks we are setting ourselves. Knowing things is essential, but it is not enough. We also need to *do* things. We need to take action. We need to implement new systems, show the members of our organisation what our vision is by living it, modelling the behaviours it needs to flourish, and actively instigating it.

Most of all, however, we need to *be*. We need to be the sort of managers, the sort of people, who work, live and breathe the spirit of the organisation's vision, and who are ready to communicate it to every member. We need to become and stay interested in the people we work with, and we need to be the sort of people who are not afraid to challenge long-held beliefs, and age-old ways of doing things. We need to be the sort of people who maintain the values that are central to the organisation's vision, and who maintain those values in the face of external or internal pressures.

Defining success

The vision of the knowledge worker is, or should be, part and parcel of feeling successful. Of course, "success" is a very personal sentiment. It is easy to identify Richard Branson or Bill Gates as successes. But what about Mother Teresa? Is she a success? The answer can only be, "yes, so course." So, clearly, the concept of success is a broad one, and there is no one single measure to determine what success is.

When one asks most people what success means to them, and how they will know when they are successful, they will say, "When I am happy, I will know that I am successful."

The fact is that success is, on a personal level, a series of emotions. It is not about how you are feeling right now, but whether there is the potential there to feel still better. The answer to feeling successful is to create a series of resourceful emotions. When one is experiencing resourceful emotions, one feels successful. For teams to be successful, they have to become able to experience the emotions that accompany success, and they will not experience them if their performance and goals are determined purely in terms of numbers. Another aspect of success is that one can never have enough of it, insofar as truly successful people are never satisfied, never sated, by the gains that they have already made. It is crucial here to draw a clear distinction between "unsatisfied" and "dissatisfied." Successful people are not *dis*satisfied, because they know that the things they want are within their grasp. They are always, however, *un*satisfied, because they know that there is more for them out there, and they want to get it. That is what gives them a reason to come to work every day.

Successful people are created to be strivers, seekers, and achievers, to be forever unsatisfied. The most successful people want a lot more than the basics of growing, living, and reproducing. They want purpose, and they are ready to work towards the goals that will give them this purpose. This is what Robert Browning had in mind when he wrote, "Ah, but a man's reach should exceed his grasp, else, what's a heaven for?"

Successful companies in today's economy are generally composed of knowledge workers, and teams of knowledge workers, who are able to access and feel resourceful emotions, who understand what their vision is, and have a clear idea of how to accomplish it, and who are able to broach the issue of how they are feeling, of how their feelings are impacting on their work, and of what they need in order to work more resourcefully and more successfully towards their personal, local, and company visions.

Finding that vision

One of the main obstacles standing between companies, their employees and the crucial vision is the widely-held theory that there is never enough time to broach issues that seem to be so much less impelling and important than immediate things, like answering emails, dealing with customers, and getting that product or this service into the public arena.

On of the best selling business books ever written is Seven Habits of Highly Effective People, by Covey. The reason why this book is still doing so well is because its message is just as relevant today as it was when the book was written. Its relevance here lies in his crucial message that it is worth finding and making time to deal with the all-important issue of identifying and creating vision within an organisation.

In his book, Covey divided tasks at hand into four quadrants, which can be depicted graphically like this:

Urgent and important   Important, but not urgent

Urgent, but not very important   Not important, and not urgent

It is not difficult to interpret this graphic. All tasks have an "urgency" quota, and all have an "importance" quota. For example, answering a time-sensitive query from a potential client who would like to make a large order is very urgent and very important, while discussing the menu for next year's Christmas staff buffet is of low urgency and is not very important.

Typically, urgency tends to trump importance in the workplace. This means that issues that are of paramount importance, but that do not necessarily have to be tackled ahead of a pressing deadline, tend to lose out. And the one that loses out most of all? You guessed right. Finding and fostering vision.

Developing staff and working on creating both company-wide and local vision is something that we never pencil into our schedule, so we end up without enough time to handle this crucial element of management, which falls firmly into the quadrant of "Important, but not urgent".

In finding vision, it is crucial to understand what category each task belongs in, to understand the role it plays in completing our mission. When this has been determined, we can make an effective choice about how we will spend our time and divide our attention.

A case in point

Once, I was working with a company, an investment house with a strong culture of hiring and firing, where every task was timed, and everything was urgent, because it was linked to the markets, and the markets do not wait for anybody. One of the employees I met was a young man called John, who was considered by management to be one of the bright young sparks of the company. John was rising rapidly up through the ranks. "John's got a rocket ship stuck to his arse," were his manager's precise, if rather inelegant words, "and his six-month appraisal is coming up. Would you like to sit in on it?"

Curious to see how the company handled management issues, I accepted the invitation, and in came John. John's boss discussed his performance with him a little, and then asked: "How do you think I think you are doing?"

John was honest. He coughed a little bit, and then said he thought that his boss was quite happy with what he was getting up to.

"Actually," the manager said. "I am very disappointed in you."

Poor John! I could see the colour draining out of his face. At the same time, I was getting confused, too. Was this not supposed to be rocket-ship boy?

"I have been watching you," the manager said. "You come in early, you do a lot of work, you are thought of highly by your team, you are always out there, going around helping them, sorting them out…but do you know, I have never once walked past your office and seen you with your feet up and your hands behind your head, doing nothing. Not *once*. I have only ever seen you doing stuff."

Well, John was seriously confused by now.

"I pay all those people out there to do stuff," his manager explained. "I pay *you* to *think*. You are a manager. I want you to solve problems before they arise. You need to think. You need to strategise."

What this insightful manager was talking about was the importance of creating vision; of doing things that may not be urgent, but that are important. Bloody important.

Coaching and developing staff, helping them to acquire their vision and participate in the vision of the company, is important, and effective managers realise this. They know that they have to put in the time caring about their employees, and interacting with them on a human level, even if that means that the sacred in-tray fills up a little, and even if it means that they have to delegate some of the authority, take some risks, or accept embracing a new approach. Setting time aside for nurturing an organisation's vision should become a regular activity, and something that often makes its way into the manager's to-do list. What is more, this is something that truly effective managers already know and put into practise. The Richard Bransons of this world do not say, when faced with the issue of connecting with employees, that they have "too much to do." Connecting in this way is even more important today than before, as employees risk becoming socially and personally isolated within their organisation, as we all spend more time interacting with a computer interface, and less with our clients and co-workers as individuals.

So, what sort of environment do we have to create in our organisations, in order for success to become real to each and every member? The answer lies in leading from a basis of clearly defined, demonstrable, and demonstrated values.

Values based leadership

Management from a basis of clear core values is the best way to consistently model to all the members of the organisation how the business would like itself to be experienced by the wider world, and by its members, and creates an environment in which useful belief systems and resourceful emotions are fostered.

When managers have to deal with a new situation, they can respond on the basis of instinct, past experience, or values. Which approach is best? Instinct is a seriously flawed approach. We have already discussed the power of the more primitive aspects of the mind and of our adrenal systems on decision making. Decisions based on instinct, on "gut feeling" are not born in the neocortex. The problem with relying on past experience is that any decision made will be heavily influenced by past context, even if experiences that have already been lived are of limited use in the type of organisation that will result if our vision is fulfilled. Beliefs, similarly, are derived from experiences that are rooted in past circumstances.

Instead, when we formulate the values that we as individuals and we as organisations would like to embody, we have a real, useful basis on which to make important decisions.

We—as individuals, as businesses and as cultures—are increasingly aware that we cannot live and work successfully in a value-free environment. We are beginning to learn that there is nothing desirable about the state. What is more, we are beginning to learn that we get out of both life and work what we put in.

If we manage and lead on the basis of firm values, our companies are more likely to succeed, and we are less likely to suffer from problems of talent retention, with all the money and time wasting that that involves. In other words, making decisions based on our values is not just nice; it makes hard-nosed business sense, and the statistics are there to prove it.

But what *are* values? We are all different, so clearly we each have different ideas about appropriate ways to behave. Different cultures also have different values, to varying degrees. How do we decide which values to bring to our organisation, and how to implement them? This is a delicate balancing act that calls not just for self-exploration, but also for sensitivity to how our social environment is evolving.

Successful organisations, today and in the future, know that self-interest is the least important quality that its managers can bring to the table. Managing from a basis of values that are good for everyone will create an organisation in which the best people want to stay and for which they will feel such loyalty that they will bring the best of their creativity and insight to work every day. Who wants to work for an organisation whose brand or reputation is one of untrustworthiness or another negative trait, however unjustified the accusation? What sort of employees is such an organisation going to end up having to hire?

Let's look at an example: McDonald's has been one of America's leading brands for more than half a century and, for decades, they had no problem recruiting excellent staff at every level, including managerial. For decades, the McDonald brand was seen as representing everything people liked about America: innovation, friendliness, accessibility, and the free market. In recent years, however, the brand appeared to no longer represent the values that talented staff liked to feel they embodied, and the company began to have difficulty finding and keeping top-level staff. In Douglas Coupland's iconic novel, Generation X, the term "McJob" was coined and was soon adopted into the popular lexicon, much to McDonald's chagrin.

McDonald's was not the only prominent organisation in such a situation. As Marquez points out, "firms with strong names are revamping their recruiting initiatives to focus more on communicating to prospects the key aspects of their corporate cultures that they believe will attract the best candidates." McDonald's set about defining qualities such as "pride" as central to the organisation's values. Similar values-exploration and promotion took place in big-name companies such as American Express, with the company spokesperson stating that, "We want candidates who, like our card members, aspire for more."

Lest anyone think that a manager's values, as displayed in the way he or she lives and works every day, are not central to how the organisation develops, many research studies have shown that, in fact, they are extremely important. Senior managers decide the company's aspirations, and must make sure that everybody is working to meet them. They must ensure that the organisation's goal and ultimate destination is not only understood by the employees, but that it is something the employees want; something that is relevant to their own personal values and goals, and something that they can relate to.

Fernandez and Hogan have devised the MVPI, the Motives, Values and Preferences Inventory. They have used it in studying how managerial skills and values interact, and they have identified "four different values clusters. Each of [which] produces a coherent, explicit managerial character. They are: the strategist, the analyst, the mentor, and the innovator."

Strategists are motivated by excitement and power, and tend to be "push" managers. What matters most to them is winning, and they tend to interact with fellow managers and with employees in a rather forceful manner. According to Fernandez and Hogan, this sort of manager tends to focus on external issues, including customers, competitors, technological advances, and market trends, and rely on employees who can handle running the daily machinations of the organisation, and who can analyse and plan on their own.

Managers who fall under the category of "analysts" tend to work towards stability and predictability, and focus on consistency and eliminating risk. They tend to spend a lot of time on developing policies and procedures, and appreciate experience over innovation.

Manager-mentors are primarily interested in collaboration, high standards and interpersonal relationships, as well as in developing employees who will be able to make decisions autonomously.

Innovators are most interested in process and change, and try to create a work environment that promotes learning and experimentation, and value most highly aggressive, independent, creative individuals.

As Fernandez and Hogan point out, these four categories are not immutable, and managers can embody different characteristics at different times. However, what is clear is that the manager's dominant values will affect the organisation at every single level. Their findings also revealed that managers' values, and how closely these values are in tune to the organisation's goals, have a much greater impact on the success of the organisation's success than their knowledge of the field. Most important is that managers show by the way they behave that they live according to their values. The point is not necessarily that one set of values is better than another, but that managers must always be consistent, because integrity and honesty are invariably held to be of the utmost importance by an organisation's members. In their words, "people will only follow the lead of individuals whose prime values align with their own."

The statistics of managing by values

In a revolutionary book entitled Built to Last, the authors Collins and Porras traced the history of eighteen major organisations, whose growth in value was a full fifteen times more than the market between 1926 and 1990. The companies will be very familiar to you, as they include American Express, Boeing, Citicorp, Ford, General Electric, Hewlett Packard, IBM, Johnson & Johnson, Marriott, Merck, Motorola, Nordstrom, Philip Morris, Proctor & Gamble, Sony, Wal-Mart, and Walt Disney.

Now, these companies do very different things, but what they all have in common is that they base their goals and their management styles on values and purpose, rather than on numbers and money-making. Making money is just one of their objectives. Fortuitously, pursuing their goals on a basis of firm values just happens to create an environment in which money is made.

The performance of any given organisation is related very closely to its ability to use the human potential within. Companies in which workers are emotionally fulfilled, and feel themselves to be secure and appreciated, can access their potential. Knowing that they are part of a larger whole that espouses meaningful value gives employees the emotional clout they need to utilise their personal reservoirs of creativity.

Measuring and monitoring results is an integral aspect of strategic management, and of realising a company's vision. Without measurement, there is no way to know how well the organisation's vision is being implemented, and with what success plans are being integrated into the organisation's way of doing things.

Above all, possessing vision, understanding and learning how to live a company's values and knowing that one's future in the company will be one in which growth and learning are assured, empowers each of an organisation's members to start becoming the best they can be.

PART THREE:

THE WAY WE WILL BE

Chapter 7)

The Votive Process: Embracing the Seventh Age of Management

B ack in the mid-nineteenth century, the notion that workers should be given perks, such as time away from loading materials, was initially considered ridiculous. Today, too many managers see investing as employees as ridiculous, too. They say things like, "We cannot afford to send that lot on a course about developing interpersonal skills when we're making so little money. We need all hands on deck right now. We have got to keep pushing the wheel!"

Just like the nineteenth century industrialists who did not realise that better working conditions led to better work, managers who fail to see the big picture do not realise that content, satisfied, fulfilled employees will work harder and, above all, will work better.

To create a new way to manage, a new way to live, we have got to look to the future and embrace a new way of management. My proposal is that the Votive Process offers a template that will help you to transform the way you work, manage and live for a future that is immeasurably better.

Of course, tearing up the rule book is not enough. We need to get way beyond shaking our heads and saying, "The way we have done things in the past is not up to scratch any more." Instead, what we have to do is find an utterly new approach, one that reflects our new ways of living and thinking, the myriad of social changes that have occurred since Scientific Management was formulated, and one that is flexible enough to help us travel into the future in organisations that work productively, and provide environments in which the best, the most talented, individuals will want to spend their time.

True north alignment

We use the term "true north alignment" to describe the situation when everyone within an organisation has a clear idea of where they are going, and why they are going there. The term is borrowed from the navigational term "true north", which refers to the position of absolute north in relation to the individual, as opposed to magnetic north, which is where the needle on a compass points. By locating true north, the navigator can make his or her way to wherever he or she wishes to go.

In the modern workplace, by identifying the parameters that mark their goals and aspirations, the individual can—or should—be able to make his or her way to wherever he or she wishes to go.

Beginning the process starts with strategic analysis. There needs to be a clear analysis of the strategic view of where the company is going. In the United Kingdom, we tend to do strategic analyses annually, whereas in the United States, where—let's be honest here—they are much better at it, they do five- and ten-year plans.

Every organisation needs to have a core set of values, and acquire a strategic view vis a vis where they are heading, and where they would like to be heading. Where is the star that will lead them to their true north?

The difference between our view at Votive and the mainstream view is that we believe that the company *as a whole* needs to be involved in this process. There has to be input from the shop floor, and everywhere else in the company. Locating true north should not be just a boardroom activity. In fact, while the boardroom might produce the final product, the discussions that go into the boardroom's decision should take place at every level within the organisation; from a much, much wider body of people than is currently the case, because the body of people are the company; the board is not the company.

People do not need to be told where they are supposed to be going. They need to be able to say, "This is a vision that we want to be part of," for reasons that they understand and appreciate. The strategic analysis experience has to be done, before or after the business of working with attitudinal change gets underway. Then, the organisation's vision has to be determined, and real vision has to be created at every single level within the business.

Development is key

A key aspect of the Votive Process is that it moves away from training to development. Our focus is on creating development, which is why we work with spaced repetition—with a learning process that exposes people to information and stimuli over and over again to create learning, until they have integrated the new knowledge and the new behaviours that accompany it. As members of the development community, we have learned that it is past time we moved beyond the accountancy paradigm to the full development of the human being within the organisation. We have to invest time, effort and money in educating and in helping people to unlearn old habits and learn new habits; habits that will be applicable in the Seventh Age of Management.

Development and training are expensive, and they take time. Some people will be tempted to cut corners, and to try to provide both within the workplace without seeking help. But effecting lasting change is difficult, and we believe that it is always necessary to seek external help in making the sort of difference that needs to be made. Attempting to do it using purely internal resources will never be adequate.

For a compound of reasons, messages received from internal resources are not received and absorbed sufficiently to create meaningful change. One of the principal reasons why this just does not work is because of the hierarchies within any organisation. Internal experts can do a wonderful job at helping people to acquire or develop skills, but invariably fall short when it comes to working with fundamental attitudinal issues and challenges—and, as we have seen, the most important changes any organisation or individual can make are in attitude.

We have already ascertained that companies need to change how they are doing things. But how *can* they? Is it even possible? How difficult will it be? In fact, the hardest part about changing the way one does things is accepting that one could use a better approach than that adopted so far. Embracing the notion of change is the most difficult part of all.

The first step in creating a new way of managing, a new set of relationships, comes with recognising that it is time to restructure and time to change priorities. Of course, nobody is claiming that it is going to be easy. In most—if not all—cases, help will have to be sought from outside, because organisations almost invariably are dealing with too much baggage to handle things effectively. Within any organisation, there is a history of doing things a certain way, there are power struggles, there are interpersonal relationships that sometimes fail to be completely frank and straightforward and there is an infinite range of already-formed habits, that are often so ingrained that only an outsider can even identify them.

Understanding the needs of knowledge workers, and learning how to manage them, calls for spending more time face-to-face with one's teams, and spending more time talking about the future, where the team is going to be, and what it will be doing, rather than focusing on the numbers that the team is going to have to crunch. It means understanding what people need, and then applying that understanding, rather taking the understanding on board, and then doing what one has always done. Above all, it means doing a lot more than reading a pamphlet about the latest management fad and holding a meeting about why it matters, without doing anything meaningful to change one's behaviour.

When it comes to making changes, behaviour speaks a great deal louder than words. What really matters is not what one *does* but how one *reacts*. Our ability to control what happens—what we experience—is limited. What we can control is our response, and how we choose to respond affects the outcome.

How can the manager foster feelings of contentment and of less or no stress in the workplace? The answer starts with communicating with the workers about their needs. It starts with getting up from behind that iconic desk, and having conversations with people not only as workers, but as human beings. It starts with understanding what employees' personal goals are, and how these goals can be realised within the context of the organisation. The more those conversations are held, the better the manager will know the workers, the more responsive they will be, and the more complete their connection with the workplace and with the company's vision. The positive emotions that will result from this change in doing things will make an enormous difference. In the knowledge that their manager, and the organisation for which they work, wants and needs them to be successful, and wants and needs to hear their positive, individual contributions, workers will feel more successful and, as a result, more driven and more focused.

The Votive Process has at its core the understanding that we need to create development, not training. You cannot train people to develop attitude in the same way they acquire skills. You cannot send them on a course and expect them to change. You need to create development, and to create development you need to have what we called "spaced repetition", in which messages are repeated over and over again until they influence the way individuals work. One challenge facing organisations committed to development is that spaced repetition can be expensive, at least if it is necessary to bring in external assistance for course after course after course. The Votive Process centres on an initiation event, when employees meet face-to-face with the external coach. This event can last for a few hours to a few days, depending on what needs to be done, and the time and resources available. This is followed by a series of PDF and audio file "drops" that are received every week, or every other week, over a period of four to eight weeks. The provision of the same message remotely in visual and audio form provides the spaced repetition that is so crucial to learning and it also matches employees' needs in terms of work and lifestyle. People are busy and they have full personal lives; this method makes it possible for them to access information on the train going home, and to listen to audiofiles on their i-pods. It facilitates learning while minimising the amount of extra time individuals need to put into it—time that would, of necessity, have to come out of their personal and family commitments.

Making the decision to change and accepting that help will have to come from outside is an important step but, clearly, it is not enough. Companies will have to follow through by investing in the changes that they have decided to make, financially, temporally, and emotionally. We invest in every aspect of our companies—the computer equipment, the physical environment, the workers' skills—and we also need to invest in vision and in creating a new system of management. We need to have faith in our vision and in our choices, and we need to understand what we will have to do to implement them. While managers who obsess about achieving success according to a narrow-minded accountancy paradigm will be disappointed, and will apportion blame when this does not happen, those who know that their vision is a good one will live and work according to it and will find that, as a result of this shift in approach, they *will* meet the numbers and they *will* grow. If that has not happened yet, it may be because not enough time has passed, or because people are not learning from their mistakes, but doing the same thing over and over. The point is that when the vision is right, and is implemented well, success will inevitably follow.

What is crucial, after you have set up an initiation session with an external management consultant and you have put the spaced repetition into action, is that all the messages that are being received are backed up within the workplace with a solid, dedicated mentoring program and a monitoring process. Of course, making sure that people are reading what they have been given to read, and doing whatever exercises they have been asked to do, could be done by somebody external to the company, but it is more efficient for this to be carried out by the managers within the organisation, who act as support, ask the questions that need to be asked, and help to develop the individuals who are working for them. This calls for creating the sort of community within the organisation that will allow a culture of development to flourish.

Manageable, measurable and monitorable results.

Crucially, managers need to know what to measure, and they need to know how to measure these key variables in relation to where the organisation has been, where it is now, and where it is heading. They need to ensure that the steps they take in both the strategic planning process and the strategic management process are flexible. We need a method of reviewing the plans and incrementally modifying them as events and environments dictate, so that at any point we know where we are going, and how we will get there. Measuring also needs to be tied to the changes that are occurring in the wider world. At the end of the learning period, after all the PDFs and audiofiles have been studied and absorbed, there needs to be what we can call a "gathering period" to analyse and see how the new technique is going. Then the programme can be repeated again. *Then* you may start to see real, lasting change.

Anyone who tells you that real change can come from going on a single course is thinking about ticking the box labelled "development" and filing the invoice. They are not thinking about real learning, because real learning calls for much repetition, because of the four steps of learning we discussed earlier, because of the habitual changes and because of the inevitable problems and hitches along the way—problems that can, with the right approach, become part of the learning process but which, if ignored, can turn everything on its head; issues of nervousness, anxiety and apparent resistance to change.

If we are going to change the culture within our organisations, we need to apply the process to a number of areas. That process can be applied to attitude, the development of a coaching culture within an organisation, presentation areas, communication strands within an organisation, our attitudes to responsibility, and so forth. The process needs to be applied not just to management but also the worker, the person on the shop floor, because everybody needs educating and developing in terms of taking responsibility, in working with their managers, and in treating them in a different, more open, more honest way. Everyone in the organisation needs to have a clear idea of where they are going.

But is it possible to focus on the things that need changing, and on how to change them, to the detriment of the organisation? Clearly, the organisation is going to have to continue producing or providing a service, even as it undergoes profound change. No company can set up an autoresponder that informs customers that, "Due to attitude training, we will be closed for six months."

Integrating change while continuing to produce or provide a service will be easier if managers have already worked at changing the organisation's culture; the underlying set of beliefs that characterise the compound of the way the organisation's members live and work within it. The status quo must already have been challenged, and a new set of cultural traits—a new set of beliefs—put in place, first in management and then by degrees in each level of the organisation. Making this change in the culture and belief system of the organisation demonstrates very clearly that this brave new world that is being posited is not a scary one, but one that will be a good place in which to work and grow.

Knocking down symbols

When the conquistadores stormed the Mexico City of the Aztecs, back in the sixteenth century, one of the first things they did was to knock down and destroy the Aztecs' public monuments to their gods and to their political heroes. They knew that by destroying the ancient culture's symbols of power and authority, they were striking a blow at its very heart. More recently, the United States army attempted to do much the same thing in Iraq when, shortly after their invasion, they set about destroying statues and images of Saddam Hussein. Conquering armies have always known that, just as important as destroying their foes' armies and bastions of power, is publicly knocking down all the symbols they hold so dear.

The Papacy of John Paul II also gives us an intriguing example of what can happen when outward symbols of authority are removed. While the conquering army typically tears down one set of symbols and replaces them with another, when John Paul II became Pope, he embarked on a brilliant strategy; that of making himself as Pope *less* dependent on external trappings of authority. Where previous Popes had been kept very much apart from their congregations, he engaged in public displays of humility, such as his famous "tarmac-kissing" every time he landed in a new country. He got up close and personal with unprecedented numbers of Catholics. Catholics felt able to communicate with their leader—the ultimate manager of their organisation—as never before.

In order to forge a new type of management, it will also be necessary to destroy or change some of the symbols of managerial authority that can come between today's managers and the effective management of knowledge workers. It will be hard for some managers to let go of things they feel they have worked long and hard for, and this is why it is always necessary to seek external help in effecting long-lasting change in this area. But it is vitally important. Removing the symbols of authority that serve as obstacles between managers and employees is especially important in medium and large organisations in which a personal relationship between senior managers and all their employees is not possible because of the numbers of people involved. However, instead of destroying one symbol of authority only to replace it with another, a more effective way of helping people to take charge of their own performance, innovation, and intelligence within your organisation is to make authority less centralised; to give each member of the organisation access to their own authority within the realm they operate in. By doing this, it becomes possible for each member of the organisation to connect in a meaningful way with the vision of the organisation, and with their personal role in fulfilling that vision.

So, what *are* the manager's symbols of authority? And what is the big deal about dismantling them?

Typically, the manager has a title and more privilege than his employees, who may even feel intimidated when they are invited inside his or her space, because that iconic environment is associated with experiences that are not pleasant: With being told that there will not be a pay increase or a Christmas bonus, with being told what to do and not asked for feedback, and so on. He or she may not realise it, but the trappings of their success all provide a message of power and authority that certainly can intimidate, and that is of very little help in promoting real, useful, meaningful communication. That will necessitate a different way of talking and relating. Managers will have to get out and talk to people more. They will have to work hard to achieve a customer-service attitude towards all their employees, and this will have to translate to every single interaction in the workplace every day. The questions that should always be at the forefront of their minds are: What does this customer need? How can I help them to achieve their goals? This approach must be pervasive throughout the organisation: The company's board should see senior management as their customers; senior management should see junior management as their customers, and so on. When literally everyone within an organisation is seen as a customer, their views, needs, and even problems are seen through a different filter. When you believe that the person working for you is a customer, you go to a much different place vis a vis how and when you interact with them. This shift in views must translate to real vision at every level of the organisation. Why should the manager's office be his or her place apart from their workforce? Why shouldn't managers work hand-in-hand with employees? Do we really want to see our managers as absolute monarchs who must always be obeyed, even when they are wrong? Is that good for employees? Is that good for managers? Is that good for organisations? Of course not. The manager's office should be simply a space where things can be kept, and which can provide privacy when this is called for. The effective managers of the corporate environment of today and the future will spend more time away from their office, out of their chair, and in the physical space of the teams they supervise. Rather than calling their employees into their space, they will go and sit beside them. They might consider simple alterations to the physical environment that will give a message of openness and accessibility, such as keeping their office door open most of the time, setting up their office on the work floor, or installing large windows in their office space, so that there is no obvious physical barrier between management and employees. There is no reason why managers should have bigger, better offices than everybody else, either. If comfort and posture are important, they are important for everybody, and the last thing an organisation needs is a manager who enjoys his comfortable office so much that he starts feeling that it is his personal den, into which he can retreat, and from which he does not have to emerge, expect for very special occasions. In the successful office of tomorrow, there will be no underlining of authority, but rather the discussion of the matters at hand, up close and personal. By showing every day and in every interaction they have with employees that they are not afraid to ask for help, managers will make asking for help—and, as a result, providing leadership when it is called for—easier for those they manage.

Making these changes—most of which are very simple—creates an utterly different dynamic, and one that is much more conducive to fostering a creative, vision-filled company environment. By interacting with one's team in such a way, the negative associations of the office are broken down and eliminated. The desk is pushed aside, the manager reveals his or her feet of clay and in doing so, real authority—the sort that is not feared but respected—emerges.

Let me give you an example. A managing director of a major organisation hired me to provide a consultancy service. While I was there, he told me about problems he was having communicating with one member of staff in particular. The situation was frustrating, because he knew that this staff member was a talented individual, but he also knew that he was, quite simply, failing to get across to him the messages that he needed to hear. Coming from outside, one of the potential barriers to communication was quite obvious to me.

"Let's try something," I suggested. "I will sit behind your desk, and you come into your office, as if you were your employee."

The manager did as I suggested. When he entered the room, he stayed in the doorway with his hand on the door handle.

"What does your office look like from that perspective?" I asked him.

"You look like you are miles away!" he said. "The desk looks like it is miles away."

Suddenly, he realised what a barrier his actual office had come to communication. As a matter of habit, this man tended to spend a lot of time behind his desk, something that was a trigger to anxiety for this particular individual.

"I am going to have to come up with a new strategy for talking to this person," he decided. In a corner of the office, there was a low coffee table with two chairs beside it, and he determined that, in future meetings with this employee, he would leave his desk and invite him to sit at the smaller table, and that he would also overcome his own personal difficulties with going to the employee's desk and talking to him there. This altered the dynamic of meetings dramatically, and for the better.

Real authority does not fear its own limitations or flinch from asking for help. Real authority is about knowing when and how to request feedback, and it also knows that there is more power in engaging people in a relationship of mutual respect than in fostering fear. It knows that customer service is not just about keeping external customers happy, but also about really listening to and dealing with the concerns of internal customers. Just as the business that does not treat its external customers with the attention to detail that they deserve quickly perishes, the business that ignores the needs of its internal customers does so at its peril. Greater performance is what happens when everyone within an organisation operates with the knowledge and security of a customer-service driven environment of management. Of course, the relationship between customer and service provider is a mutual one. Customers must also bring something to their side of the bargain. What external customers bring is their wallet and the willingness to buy a product or service, and then use that product or service for the purpose it was designed for. Coming in and trashing the shop, grabbing the goods and running or arriving at the bus stop after the bus has left are not acceptable ways for the customer to fulfil his side of the bargain. Being a customer is a role that involves certain rules and responsibilities. Similarly, within the customer-service driven workplace, employees cannot sit back and relax; they have to fulfil their side of the bargain. They have to be honest, true and hard-working.

Embracing the different roles of management

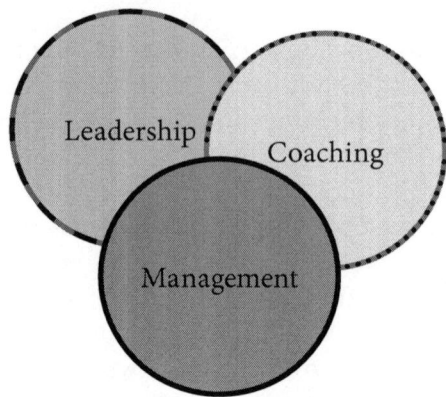

The manager as, well, manager

The first and simplest aspect of the manager's job is management; overseeing the nuts and bolts of the business, making sure that services or products are delivered satisfactorily and on time, and so forth. This is what is often referred to as "process management" and which we can also call, more colloquially, "getting the job done." These are tasks that all managers are familiar, with and that most of them spend the majority of their time doing. In this role, the manager's task is the nuts-and-bolts one of making sure that the organisation's products and services are being provided as they should, with no major hitches or delays along the way.

The beauty of working within an organisation in which values and vision are placed centre-stage is that, while ultimate responsibility for ensuring that the organisation does what it is supposed to be doing rests on the shoulders of management, at every level people will be coming up with the goods and giving it all they have got, because being creative, being innovative, and being responsible will have been accepted as core values of the organisation. Everyone will know what their responsibility is, and ensuring that they fulfil it will be very important to them.

The manager as leader

The role of the manager is, or should be, three-fold. It involves leadership, coaching and management. Most of the qualities of leadership, which include strategy and vision, can be filed in that important but non-urgent box that we mentioned above, when we discussed Covey's quadrants of urgency. The manager-as-leader must focus on issues such as strategy and vision; long-ranging, all-encompassing aspects of management that will impact on the organisation at every level, and throughout the course of its existence. What makes a real leader is nothing to do with having a more expensive suit, a bigger salary, or a fancier office. The manager as leader has convictions and a vision that are clearly defined. He or she is someone who is not afraid to stand up for what they believe in. The leader does not shirk from asking for help, but similarly is not afraid to follow vision and conviction through every single day. The manager as leader will be someone who is respected by employees, because they know that he or she works hard to embody the values that he or she would like to see embedded in the organisation. The manager as leader inspires respect, but not fear. The manager as leader offers trust, and receives it in return.

So, what should managers do in order to acquire the leadership position that is a part of their role? The answer starts with beliefs, with inspecting one's own beliefs, ensuring that they are in sync with the organisation's goals and compatible with its values. Do the manager's performance and his or her relationship with other members of the organisation reflect these beliefs, every single day? What needs to be changed to make this the case?

The manager as coach

"Coaching" is a buzz word that is bandied about a lot, and many, if not most, managers will have attended short courses on how to coach in the workplace. The problem is that, without addressing the fundamental structure and culture of the workplace, the messages taught on these courses can only be imperfectly implemented, at best. All businesses that wish to succeed have to accept a culture of coaching that goes way beyond lip-service. The role of coach is also, of course, crucial. As coach, the manager's job is to help the individuals and the teams in the business become all they can be. It is to assist them in their development within the context of the business and, as they become personally and professionally enriched, to help them to contribute to the company's success. Many of us will have had relatively little experience in the workplace of managers as coaches, and it might seem difficult to find a model for how we should integrate this aspect into ourselves as managers. Looking outside the world of work may help in finding useful models. These could include teachers or sports coaches or even members of one's family. Can you think of someone who helped you be the best you could be? Whatever the arena, the role of a good coach is to help people access the best within themselves, not by threatening them with the terrible things that will happen if they do not or by insisting that they complete an arbitrary number of tasks within a specific amount of time, but by showing them how strong they can be and how much aptitude they have. The manager as coach knows that everyone is different, and spends the necessary time getting to know each person so as to help them to tap into their own latent abilities. The manager as coach engages their staff by asking questions and by expecting and welcoming honest answers to them. The manager as coach will, in turn, give honest, frank answers to the questions that they are asked. In so doing, they understand that they will need to be able to step away from the label of "boss", because the person who is seen as an individual who only cares about boxes being ticked and accountancy paradigms being satisfied will also be seen as someone who is difficult to approach and difficult to engage with. A good coach ensures that personal performances will always continue growing stronger, because abilities are not exploited once, but nurtured and encouraged to grow. The manager as coach understands that management is less about the manager than the team, that difficulties at work also represent opportunities to learn and that success should be acknowledged and rewarded. The manager as coach understands the value of positive reinforcement. Above all, the manager as coach understands that coaching is something that you are, rather than something that you do.

Accessing power

One of the most important tasks to accomplish in the workplace is the enablement of everyone within it to access their particular power within the organisation. Clearly, management has power, but what is less obvious is the power wielded by people at every level. Positional power typically refers to senior management, but there are also qualities such as knowledge power, personal power, relationship power, and task power, as discussed by management writer Ken Blanchard.

Knowledge power is derived from the things the individual knows about or knows how to do. A computer technician has knowledge power, insofar as he knows how to fix an organisation's computers when they are down, install programs, and so forth. Personal power is one's ability to interact with others, and explain key issues and responsibilities. Relationship power derives from the ability to form and maintain good working relationships within one's organisation, or with other people who are helpful to the organisation or to one's personal career progress. Task power is derived from the responsibility for overseeing tasks that must be taken care of if an organisation is to function well; typical activities for employees like secretaries, archivists, and personal assistants.

Within any given organisation, different people have different sorts of power; often several at the same or at different times. Helping them to understand that, while their manager has positional power over them, they are powerful within their own realm, can make all the difference.

Something else that helps people to access their power is a focus on performance development, rather than performance management, performance management being the focus in most organisations today. The message that employees need to receive every day is that their manager's prime interest in them is to help them to develop as professionals and as individuals. Development is key.

Being consistent

One area where there should definitely be no surprises is the field of management. Managers have a duty to be absolutely consistent, all day, every day, especially when it is question of the human-to-human interface. The members of an organisation have a right to know what is going on and what to expect. If an organisation is facing the need to make some of its members redundant, the loss of a job should never come as a surprise to those who have to leave. Nobody should attend their performance appraisal to learn for the first time about issues that need to be addressed; if praise or constructive advice needs to be given, this is something that they should have already heard about in the context of carrying out their everyday duties. Appraisals should not be an annual event. First of all, employees should be receiving clear, consistent feedback about their performance every single day, as well as regular appraisals in which they—their needs as internal customers—are discussed in a focused way. Currently, many organisations hold employee appraisals just once a year. To say that this is not nearly enough is a serious understatement. Now, I am not saying that these appraisals need to be formal events. What matters is that the information about what needs to be done, and how people can be helped to achieve it, is allowed to be passed freely between employee and manager within the framework of a customer-service based relationship. Even when external factors create surprise—buildings are damaged in a storm, an act of terrorism rocks the stock market and shares tumble in value, or a flu epidemic sees 40% of the workplace at home in bed—the way in which the organisation's managers react to the new set of circumstances should be entirely consistent with the culture of management that they have fostered.

Getting everyone involved

One of the axioms from Stephen Covey's work is that planning should be done with the end in mind. At its most basic, that is what vision is about. The questions we need to ask are: Where is all this work I am doing going to get me? What is it for?

Because of the way businesses are organised today, a lot of the planning that is carried out at management level is done in the opposite way. The questions that are asked are. "So, where are we now?" "What will we be doing in five years' time?" "What will we do next year?"

Planning needs to be a continuous process, and it needs to be a process in which everybody in the organisation is involved. Yes, everybody! That means not just senior, middle and junior management. It means all of that…and then everybody else too.

At the moment, the typical scenario is that management devises a plan, and employees are measured against the plan. If the plan says, "We will be producing 500 crates of X product every week in six months!" this is the criterion against which the company's performance is measured.

A vision-sensitive approach to planning understands that a plan is organic; it should be something that is revisited, renewed, and revamped every time the situation changes. Rather than engraving our plans in metaphoric stone, we need to conceive of a living cycle of plans, each of which is created as the preceding plan reaches its conclusion. What is more, planning should always be a company-wide activity, with company-wide participation. Planning should never be merely the realm of the boss or the board of management. This does not mean that every single meeting has to be attended by every single worker, but that elements of the company's vision should be filtered down to every level of the business, and decided at that local level. Within certain parameters, each team should be given as much freedom and potential for developing their own plan, their own vision, as possible.

The difference that we are talking about here is the difference between strategic planning and long-term planning. Long-term planning is based on data and numbers, based on an organisation's history. It does not focus on sustainable change and it does not incorporate the issue of values. Strategic planning, on the other hand, derives from the organisation's values, and determines not just where it wants to go in terms of output and profits, but about how it wants to grow and develop as an organic entity that embodies those values and that vision.

Effective strategic planning involves posing questions about the organisation, answering those questions and using the questions as guides towards future results. According to Cox, the three basic questions that any organisation needs to ask itself are as follows:

- ❖ Where are you going?

- ❖ What is the environment?

- ❖ How do you get there?

Strategic planners understand that the environment changes, and that plans will have to be flexible. For example, a long-term plan might say, "We will increase output by 5% every six months!" That is all well and good. But what if the organisation's currency is devalued? What if the economy slows down or picks up? What if the technologies used in the organisation become obsolete? Strategic planning accepts that plans and approaches will have to change as the environment changes. Behind every successful strategic plan there is support; support for managers within the organisation, who have to implement the plan with their employees and support for the employees whose work will have to be moulded by the emerging circumstances. Strategic management is values-driven. If the company's core value is: "We provide a good service at reasonable cost," everything that organisation does has to bear this value in mind, even as currencies change, competitors emerge and market conditions continue to evolve.

Getting rid of labels

In today's workplace, there is a tendency that derives from our accounts-focussed approach, to pigeonhole people very quickly, leading to what is really the ultimate self-fulfilling prophecy. Because we measure, or attempt to measure, workers' results in terms of numbers, we are unable to see the whole person, and we create a sort of self-fulfilling prophecy about them that sells everybody short. We create a belief system about everyone we meet, and then construct a series of behaviours towards them that endorse those beliefs. In other words, if we decide that Martin is a bit of an idiot, we treat him with disrespect and, seeing how he is viewed in his workplace, he responds by, well, being a bit of an idiot.

I have a friend who left school at fifteen and worked as a brickie for about ten years. When he was in his mid-twenties, he took a degree with the Open University. In his thirties, he did an MBA. Nigel is now a partner with one of the "big four" consultancy firms. The only give-away as to his past on the building site is that, in summer, he rolls up his shirtsleeves to reveal a fine set of tattoos. Anyone looking at Nigel when he was nineteen or twenty would have seen an amiable but not particularly academic fellow. Too many would have assumed that he was always going to be amiable, but not particularly academic. In fact, Nigel was not a good candidate for university and a job in a consultancy firm when he was nineteen, because that was just not the place he was at right then. He was young, he was working on the building sites, and he was having a good time. But people change. Nigel changed. What was right for him when he was nineteen was not right for him when he was twenty-five and not right for him when he was forty. Fortunately, Nigel did not believe the label that others had stuck on his head; the one that read, "Once a brickie, always a brickie."

In order to be a coach, managers need to remove the invisible labels that they have stuck onto everybody's heads. This may sound easy, but it is not, because it calls for questioning one's own ego, dismantling the hierarchical view of management and accepting that the team will see one as—horror of horrors—a fully rounded human individual, with all the frailties, strengths, and flaws that that involves. Most of all, it calls for the removal of the label from one's own head: the label that reads "boss." The "boss" label, displayed in a thousand turns of phrase, in body language and in general attitude, says to employees louder than words: "I want you to sit and wait for me to tell you what to do." It also indicates that this is a person who will tend to label others, and this will make it difficult for employees to approach them and say, "Guess what, I cannot do this," or, "I am not very good at this, I need some help," because they know that they are putting themselves at risk of being labelled and thus potentially damaging their career within the organisation.

Removing labels—those of managers and those of employees—enables the individuals within a company to interact with one another in a much more empathetic way. Does this make us more vulnerable? In one way, yes. It means letting people inside our emotional space much more than before. But in other ways, it makes us stronger. It makes it possible for us to shift beliefs, to focus on positive change, and to change the very nature of people as managers and as employees. It makes it possible for us to move beyond the roles that we and everyone else have assumed to be immutable and to become much more than we thought possible.

In 1988, a new term was added to the lexicon of business writing: The "Pygmalion effect". The Pygmalion effect refers, in business, to the way in which managers create the sort of people they expect to have working for them by having expectations of those people, and by behaving towards them in a manner that is consistent with those expectations. Invariably, people pick up on these expectations and then perform accordingly or, as Livingston said, "The way managers treat their subordinates is subtly influenced by what they expect of them." The manager who has low expectations of the people who work for him, "cuts deeply into their self-esteem and distorts their image of themselves as human beings," while the one who skillfully communicates his high expectations of them will see that, "their self-confidence will grow, their capabilities will develop and their productivity will be high."

Being prepared to learn

As well as accepting that we have to "de-label" ourselves and others, we also have to be prepared to deal with the fact that new behaviours will take a little while to perfect. Of course, I do not mean that we should accept that our goals may sometimes be unreachable, but that we need to accept the possibility of showing the world that it is not always possible to get everything completely right the first time. We need to banish such unhelpful phrases as, "I have tried this stuff before and it has not worked." That may be true, but if you have only tried to make changes one, two, or three times before, it really does not mean anything. Not getting it quite right one, two, or three times certainly does not imply failure. Implementing changes means being consistent and learning from each experience in order to develop from it. Without change, there is atrophy. Without change, there is no potential to grow in the future. Coaches need to be able to see people—including themselves— not in terms of their past performance but of their future potential. Past performance is no indicator of what you can do in the future, and being prepared to learn is the most important ingredient in creating growth, together with becoming able to trust workers to do what they know best, while creating a mental environment that pulls employees and management closer together. Questioning fundamentally challenges not just one's own but also one's employees' beliefs, helping to build a dynamic of healthy change in the workplace. A resource that cannot be skimped on when one wants to promote a learning environment is time. You are just going to have to be prepared to give learning new ways of doing things all the time it takes, without taking shortcuts.

Addressing work/life issues

The area of balancing work and life is one in which great progress has been made in recent years. To borrow a phrase you may have heard before, much has been done, and much remains to be done. Respecting employees' needs to have a life outside work does not mean expecting less of them, or accepting that they work less hard, but it does mean being open to the possibility that some employees may job share, may work part time for a while or may need the flexibility of working from home periodically. A manager for BT I know was promoted recently. He was very happy, but before he accepted the promotion, he asked if he could leave the office early just one day a week to pick his children up from school; this would be Daddy's special day with the kids. His request was granted, and he went on to accept the promotion. The result was not a reduction in the amount of work he did, because he was able to come in earlier or leave later on other days, or take work home. Instead, BT's flexibility towards this manager's personal needs was rewarded with his loyalty and commitment to the organisation.

The manager of the future

All of the manager's roles—leader, coach and manager—are equally important to the successful functioning of the company and the healthy development of the individuals and teams within the company, but what currently happens is that the role of management tends to expand until it consumes almost all of the manager's time and energy, leaving little space for the strategic, creative side; for the vision. Very little is spent on developing the staff as human beings. Little by little, despite the best of intentions, managers spend less and less time developing themselves as leaders and as coaches. The harder they work at overseeing the daily production of the organisation, the more they feel that there just is not enough time to focus on those crucial elements of their role.

Businesses today already use appraisals, and these are often passed off as coaching. However, in order to really coach someone in a meaningful way, to help them develop within their role in a company and become the best they can be, managers need to go to them, sit with them and get to know them on a personal level. For their part, they have to know that they can feel free to be open and honest about their performance, about how and where they feel they are doing well, and how and where they feel they need more help.

Currently, it is not always wise in the corporate environment to be completely honest about areas that could do with some extra support or encouragement, and the feedback that many workers give their managers is effectively useless, because they are unable to admit, "I am not doing so well here. I could do with some help." Why? Because our managers are typically obsessed with numbers. They do not want to hear Kevin or Margaret saying, "You know, I am not very good at this." For their part, Kevin and Margaret know that, if they do not want their knuckles rapped, they had better stay quiet about the things that they are finding difficult. They know that their manager has the key to promotions, raises and preferential treatment, and they also know that he has the key to the axe. The problem here is that the roles of leadership and coaching are, in the current environment, at odds with the role of manager. To coach and lead, we need to respect and observe openness, while contemporary management is process-oriented; it is about ticking boxes and keeping the accountant happy.

Coaching in the context of the enlightened workplace will not be about "doing" something, but about "being" something. The best managers are not managers who "do" coaching, but coaches who do management. Their employees see them as coaches and mentors, but know that there will be times when they have to go into management mode. They know that these are people who can be approached. The manager who shows, day in, day out, that all he really cares about are numbers, and then wanders around one day a year saying, "I am coaching you now. Tell me your problems," will not receive very much useful feedback.

Moving on up

In the past, as we have seen, management was all about dominating the workers, keeping them nervous, hardworking, and motivated by dangling the fear of losing their job in front of them. Latterly, the move has been towards compromise and integration, and over the course of the last century, we have been realising that we need to learn how to compromise and integrate. Various attempts have been made to create a new way of interacting for management and workers, but we have been stuck with operating within the same tired old management paradigm. Now, we can get rid of it. We can decide to move forward in a way that will make our work environments, our profit margins, and our lives better in ways too numerous to count.

Over a hundred years ago, Frederick Taylor revolutionised the workplace by showing managers that workers were more efficient and worked harder when their personal needs for rest were taken care of. Nowadays, although we do not all quite realise it, we are on the cusp of new revolution; one that will create change that is just as extraordinary, far-reaching and important.

Welcome to the future.

References

Anderson Cameron and Berdahl, Jennifer L. (2002). The Experience of Power: Examining the Effects of Power on Approach and Inhibition Tendencies, Journal of Personality and Social Psychology.

Chiswick, Barry (2003). Jacob Mincer, Experience and the Distribution of Earnings, Institute for the Study of Labour. Retrieved from: ftp://repac.iza.org/RePEc/discussionpaperdp847.pdf

Barrett, Richard (April 1997). Liberating the Corporate Soul, Article for American Management Assocation's Human Resources Newsletter.

Becker, Gary (1964). Human Capital, a Theoretical and Empirical Analysis, with Special Reference to Education. National Bureau of Economic Research.

Below, Patrick with Moore, Jim (2003). The CEO Challenge, Insight Publishing.

Blanchard, Ken et al (2006). Self Leadership and the One Minute Manager, Harper Collins Publishers.

Boyatzis, R. E. (1999). From a Presentation to the Linkage Conference on Emotional Intelligence, Chicago, IL.

Boyatzis, R. (1982). The Competent Manager: A Model for Effective Performance. New York: John Wiley and Sons.

Carlzon, Jan (1989). Moments of Truth, Collins.

Chandler, Alfred D., Jr. (1988). Origins of the Organization Chart, Harvard Business Review 88:2, (March/April).

Cherniss, Cary and Goleman, Daniel. (n.d.) Bringing emotional intelligence to the Workplace: A technical report issued by the Consortium for Research on emotional intelligence. Retrieved from www.eiconsortium.org

Collins, Jim and Porras, Jerry (2002). Built to Last: Successful Habits of Visionary Companies, Collins.

Covey, Stephen R. (1990). The Seven Habits of Highly Effective People: Powerful Lessons in Personal Change, Free Press.

Cox, Bruce D. (2005). Elements of Strategic Planning; Methods, Metrics and Concepts for Building Dynamic Strategic Planning Processes. Connected; Newsletter of the Facility Management Knowledge Facility.

Davis, Albie M. (1997). Liquid Leadership: The Wisdom of Mary Parker Follett "A Leadership Journal: Women in Leadership--Sharing the Vision," Vol. 2, No. 1.

Delude, Cathryn M. (2005). Brain Researchers Explain why Old Habits Die Hard, News Offices, Massachusetts Institute of Technology.

Drucker, Peter (1996, orig. 1959). Landmarks of Tomorrow: A Report on the New "Post-Modern" World, Transaction Publishers.

Drucker, Peter (2000) Managing Knowledge Means Managing Oneself, Leader to Leader. 16: 8-10.

Drucker, Peter (November 2001). The Next Society, Economist.

Fernandez, Jorge E., Hogan, Robert T. (Winter 2002). Values-based leadership, The Journal for Quality and Participation.

Garvin, Tom, 54 (2005). Preventing the Future: Why was Ireland so poor for so long? Gill and Macmillan.

Gerstner, Louis V. (2002). Who Says Elephants Can't Dance? HarperBusiness.

Goleman, D. (1996). Emotional Intelligence: Why it can Matter More Than IQ. London: Bloomsbury.

Goleman, D. (1998). Working with Emotional Intelligence, New York, Bantam.

Griswald Wesley S. (1963). A Work of Giants: Building the First Transcontinental Railroad, New York, McGraw-Hill Book Company,

Hirshleifer, David and Welch, Ivo (June 2001). An Economic Approach to the Psychology of Change: Amnesia, Inertia and Impulsiveness, Yale International Center for Finance Working Paper no. 00-47.

Hustad, Wiggo (1999). Expectational Learning in Knowledge Communities, Journal of Organizational Change Management, Vol. 12 No. 5.

Jordan, Peter J. (2004). Dealing with Organisational Change: Can Emotional Intelligence Enhance Organisational Learning? International Journal of Organisational Behaviour Volume 8, No. 1.

Kanigel, Robert (1997). The One Best Way: Frederick Winslow Taylor and the Enigma of Efficiency. New York: Viking.

G. G. Kolden (1986). "Change in early sessions of dynamic therapy: Universal processes and the generic model of psychotherapy," Journal of Consulting and Clinical Psychology 54 (1986): 27-31.

Kuhn, Steven L. and Mary C. Stiner (2006). What's a Mother to Do, The Division of Labor among Neanderthals and Modern Humans in Eurasia, Current Anthropology 47:6.

Livingston, J. Sterling (1998). Pygmalion in Management, Harvard Business Review. (September-October), pp. 121-130.

Marquez, Jessica (March 2006). When Brand Alone isn't Enough, Workforce Management.

Mayer, J.D. & Salovey, P. (1993). The Intelligence of Emotional Intelligence. Intelligence, 17, 433-442.

Mayer, J. D. & Salovey, P. (1997). What is Emotional Intelligence? In P. Salovey & D. Sluyter (Eds). Emotional Development and Emotional Intelligence: Implications for Educators (pp. 3-31). New York: Basic Books.

McClelland, D. C. (1999). Identifying competencies with behavioral-event interviews. Psychological Science, 9(5), 331-339.

McKensie Quarterly (July 2006). Organizing for successful change management: A McKinsey Global Survey, Web exclusive.

Miller, W. R. Benefield, R. G. and Tonigan, J. S. (1993) Enhancing Motivation for Change in Problem Drinking: A Controlled Comparison of Two Therapist Styles, Journal of Consulting & Clinical Psychology, 61: 455-461

Mincer, Jacob (1958). Investment in Human Capital and Personal Income Distribution. Journal of Political Economy. Vol. 66, 281-302.

Organisation of Economic Co-operation and Development (2004). Developing High Skilled Workers; Review of Canada.

Schultz, T. W. (1961). Investment in Human Capital. The American Economic Review 1(2), 1-17.

Smith, M. K. (2002) Mary Parker Follett and informal education, the Encyclopaedia of Informal Education, http://www.infed.org/thinkers/et-foll.htm.

Stanford, Craig B. (1999). The Hunting Apes: Meat Eating and the Origins of Human Behavior, Princeton University Press.

Weber, Max (1947). The Theory of Social and Economic Organization. Translated by A. M. Henderson & Talcott Parsons, The Free Press.

Whitmore, John (2002). Coaching for Performance: Growing People, Performance and Purpose, Nicholas Brealey Publishing.

Woolridge, Adrian (2006). The Battle for Brainpower. The Economist.

About the Author

K eith Stanton grew up and attended secondary school in Leeds. On completing school in 1981, he attended the Royal Military Academy at Sandhurst where he joined the Prince of Wales's Own Regiment of Yorkshire. After serving in Norway, Berlin, Northern Ireland and Uganda, he left the Army as a Captain and Adjutant in 1991.

Civilian life brought Keith to the financial services industry. After a brief stint in consultancy he joined Yorkshire Bank in 1993, and became the Financial Services District Manager responsible for 92 branches in the Midlands.

In 1998, Keith embarked on a new career as a coach and platform speaker, initially freelance and latterly with the Si Group, providing speaking engagements in the US, the UK and Europe, South Africa, South America and Far East. In the course of the last nine years, he has worked with many blue chip organisations as well as Premiership level sports teams, World Cup and Gold Medal winning individuals, including Deloitte, HSBC, Johnson & Johnson, Novo Nordisk, NHS, Cap Gemini, Dublin Bus, Experian, Invesco, Merril Lynch, Her Majesty Courts Service, Maritime & Coastguard Agency, Orange, Royal Mail, The Disney Corporation and Reuters.

Now the founding member and Director of Votive Ltd., a leadership consultancy dedicated to creating lasting change within the corporate market place, Keith is dedicated to his process, The Votive Process, which guarantees lasting change within the corporate function; in attitudes, motivation, leadership, culture, coaching, presenting with impact, communication or personal development.

1611968R0

Printed in Great Britain
by Amazon.co.uk, Ltd.,
Marston Gate.